ZANDER CAN!

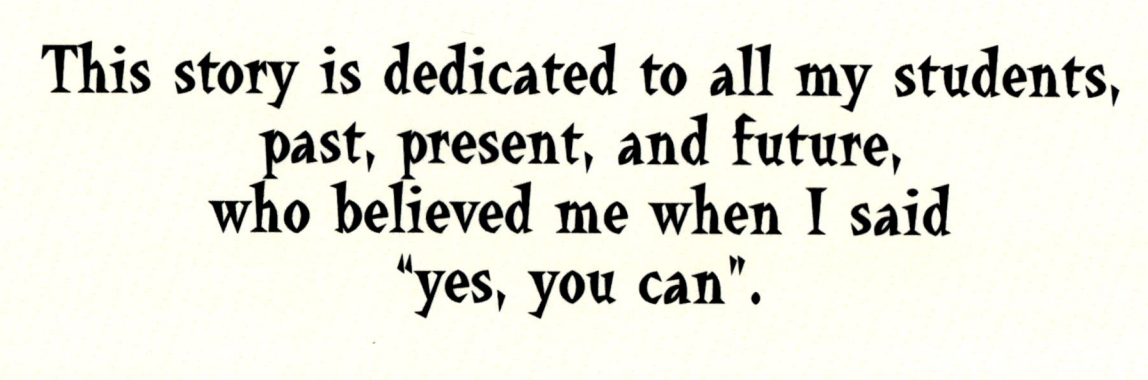

This story is dedicated to all my students,
past, present, and future,
who believed me when I said
"yes, you can".

To my daughter, Grace,
the best thing that ever happened to me,

I love you most
and keep being amazing.

by Karen Saunders Ryan

Illustrated by
Basil Zaviski

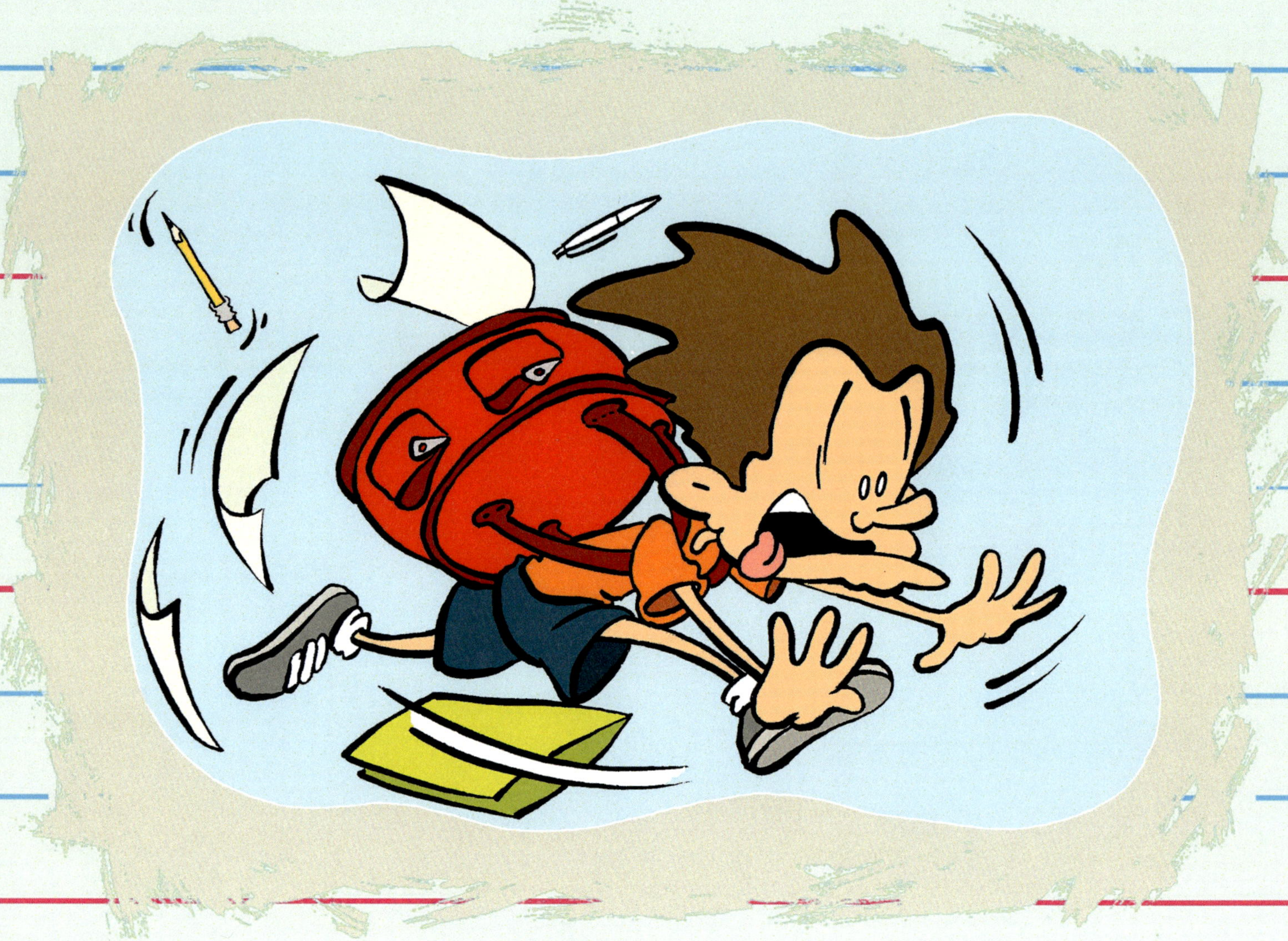

Zander couldn't wait for school to start!

He knew he was going to be the BEST at everything.

"My heart is beating in my chest,

I'm thrilled to show that I'm the best!"

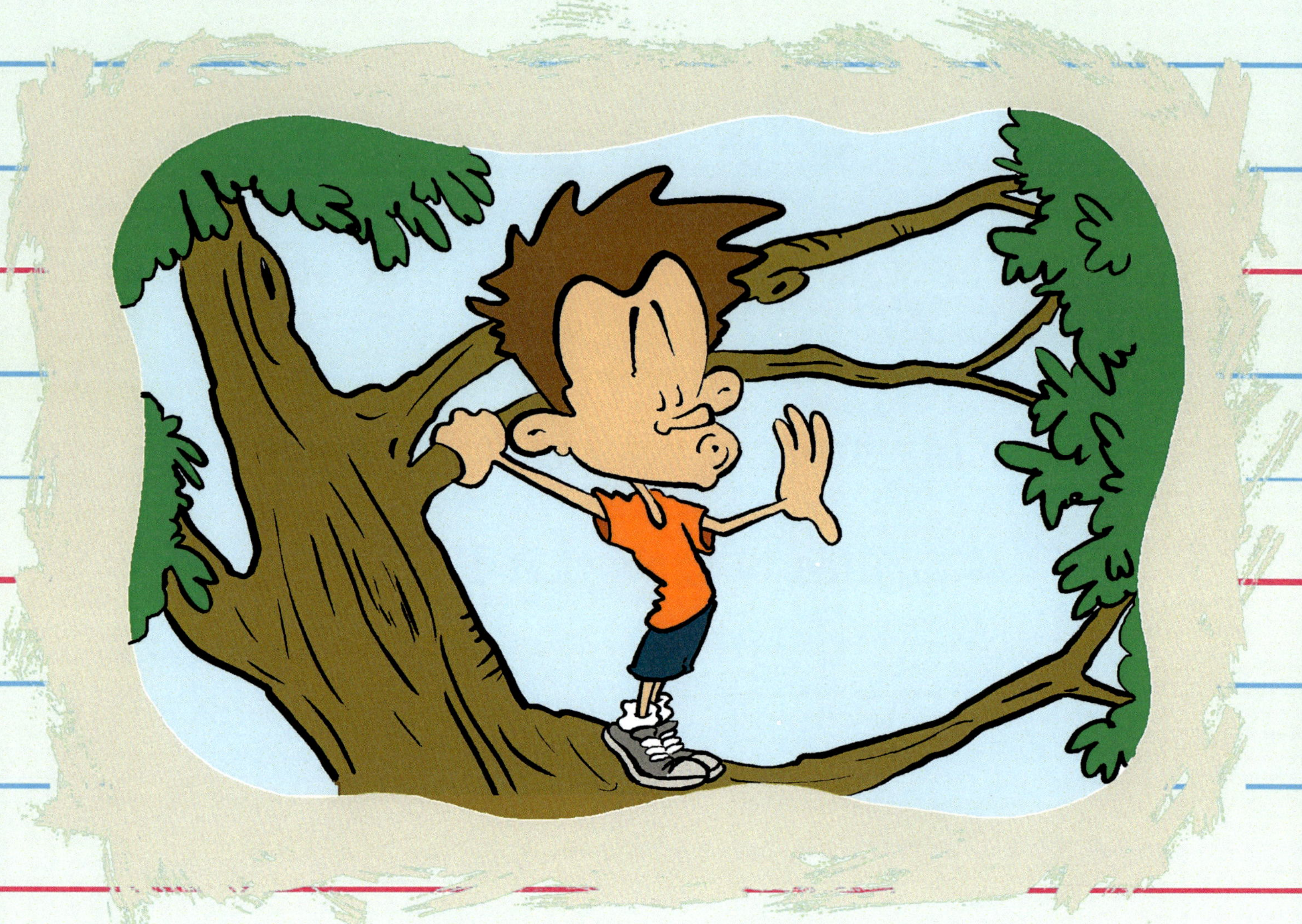

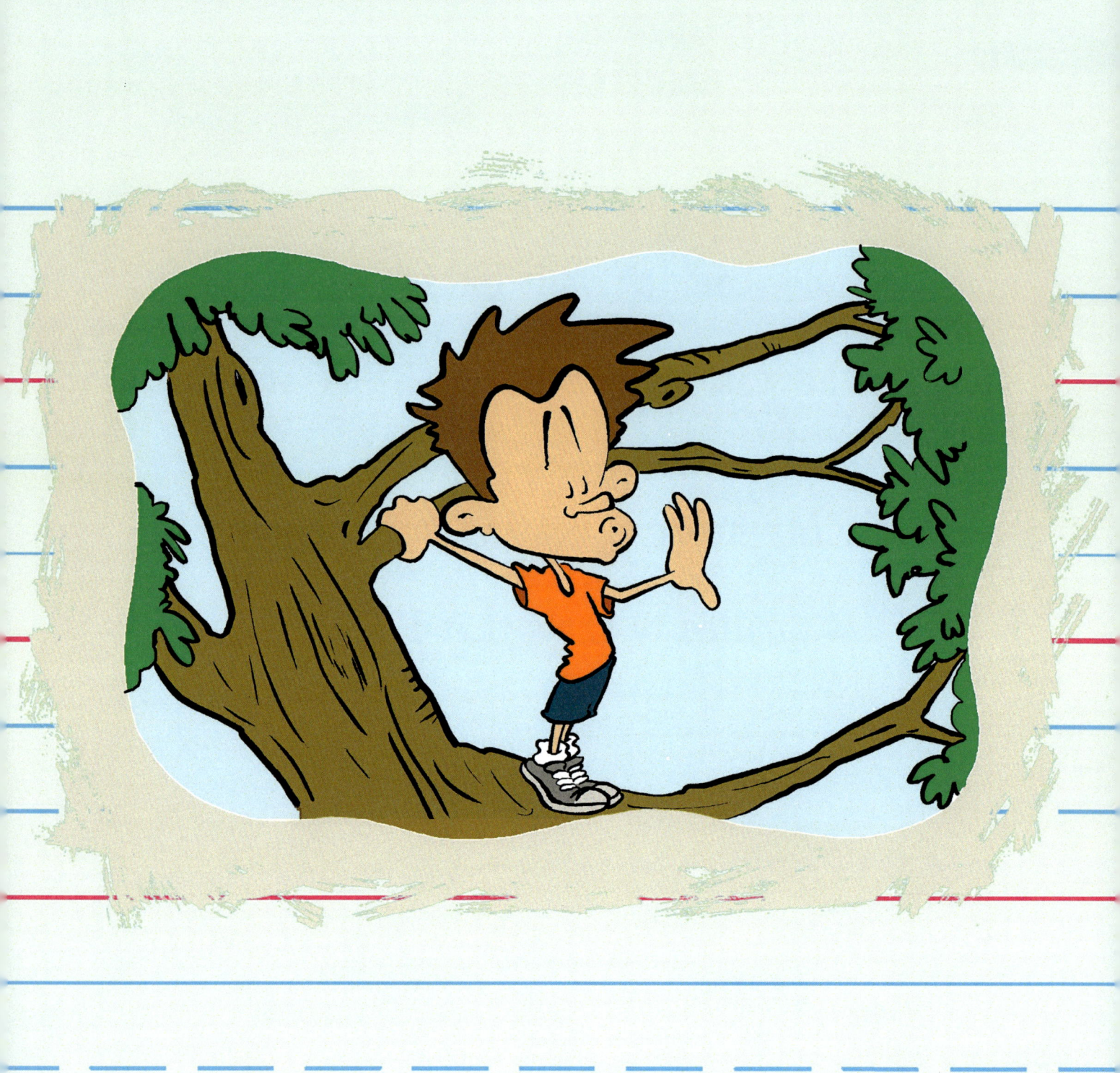

He was really good

when it came to climbing trees.

His nimble feet and agile hands

placed his head up in the breeze.

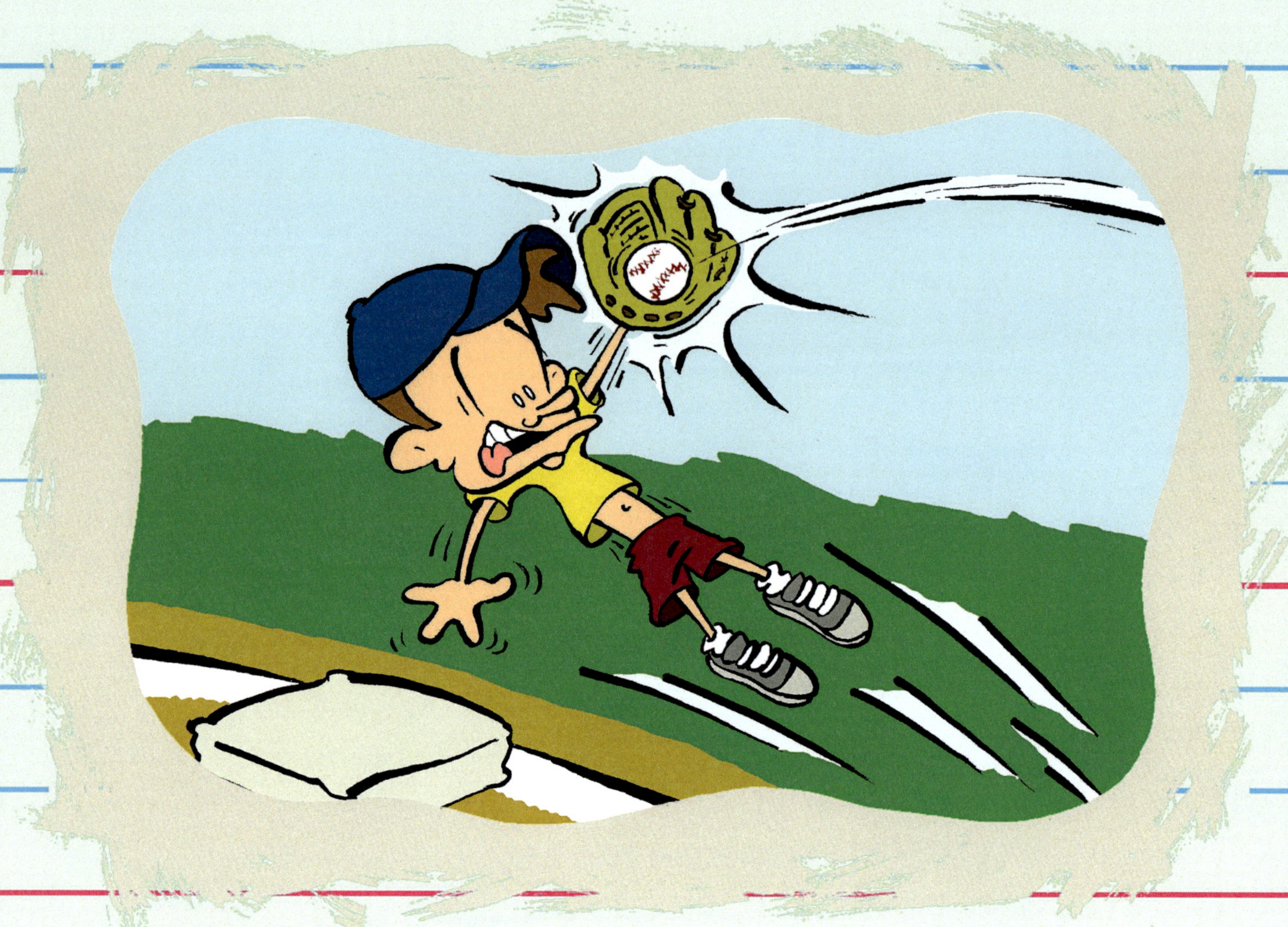

He could catch a ball AND tag a runner out.

Believing in himself, left very little doubt.

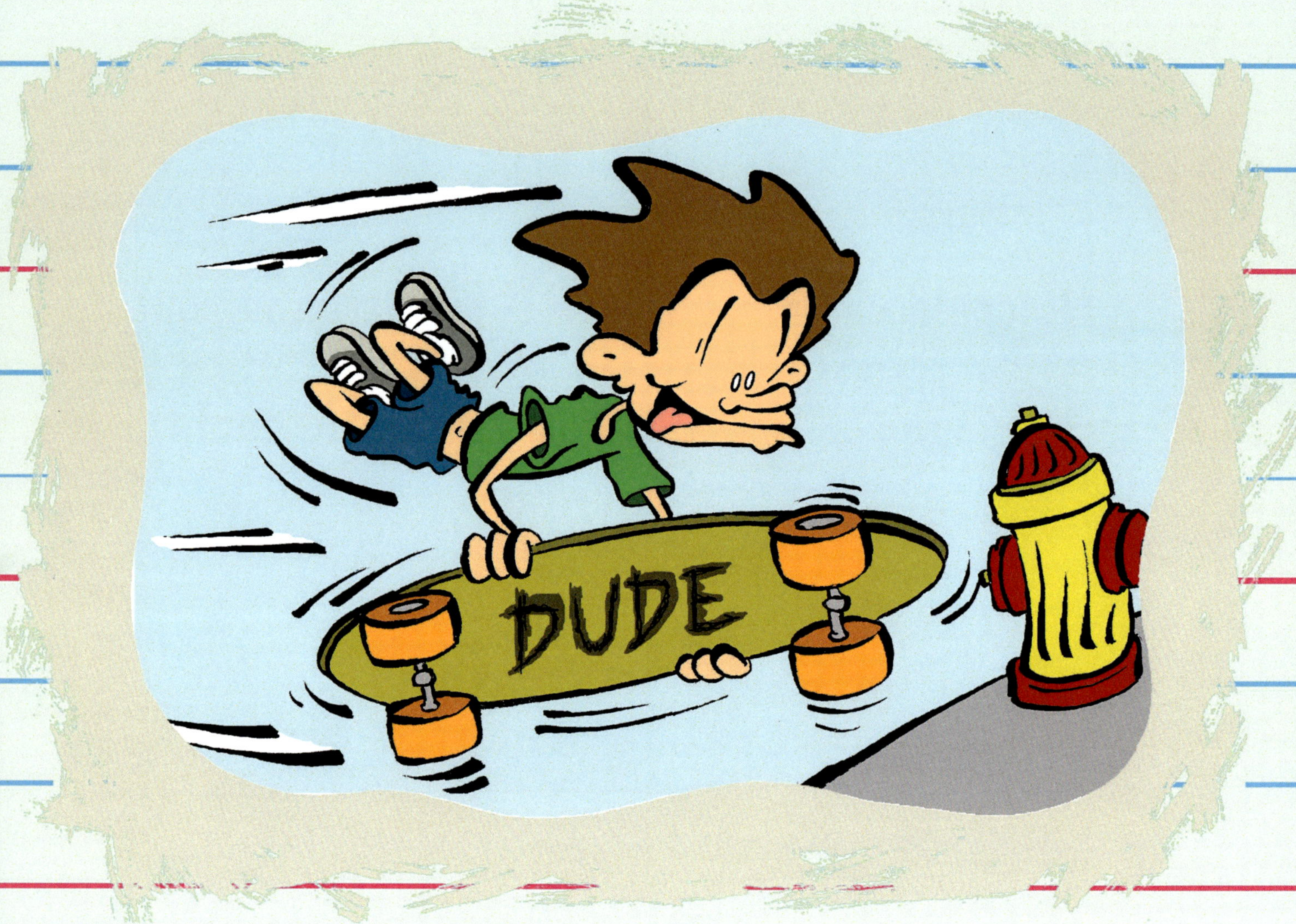
DUDE

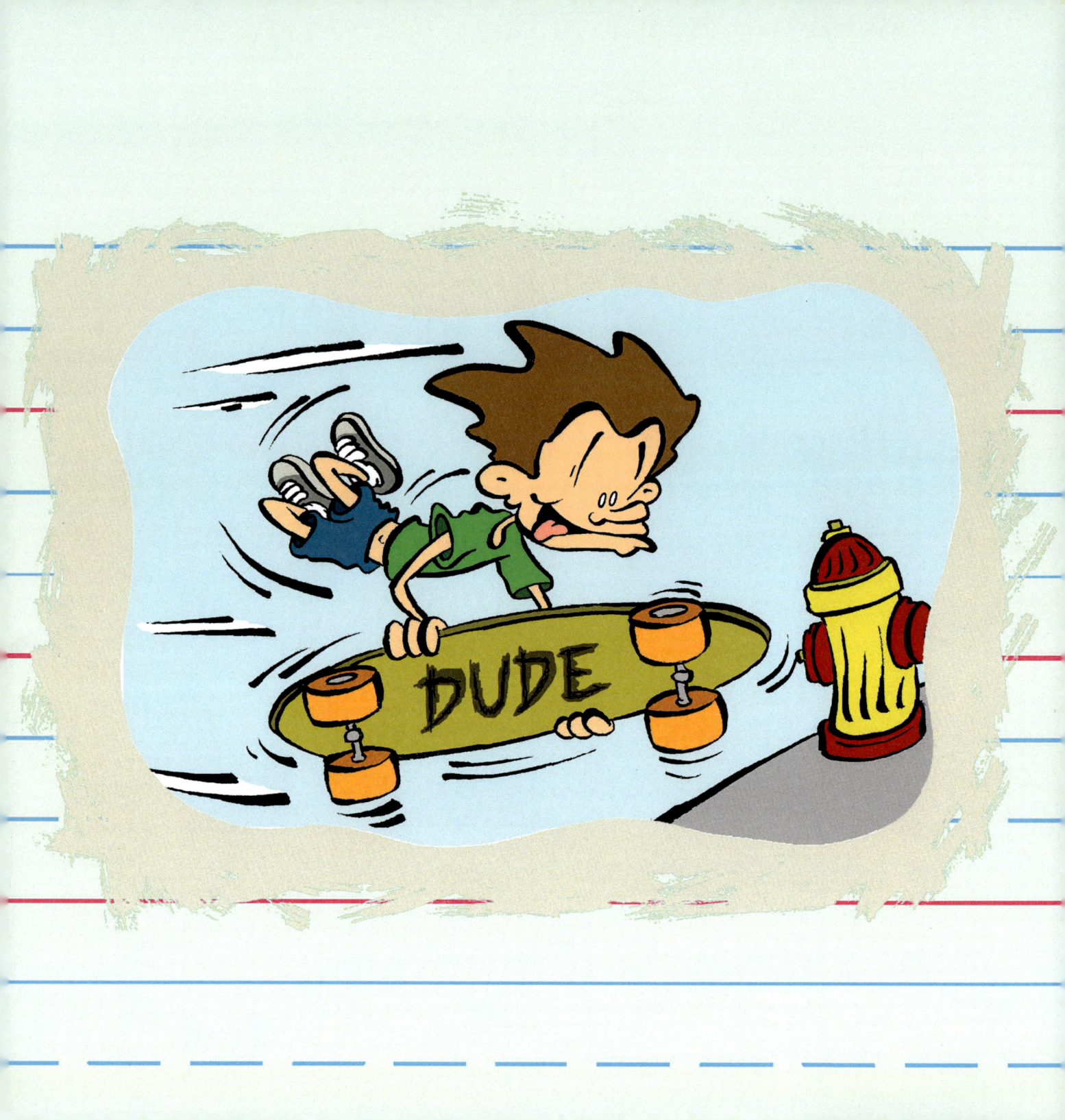

He was totally awesome at doing flips on his board.

With confident strides, he simply soared.

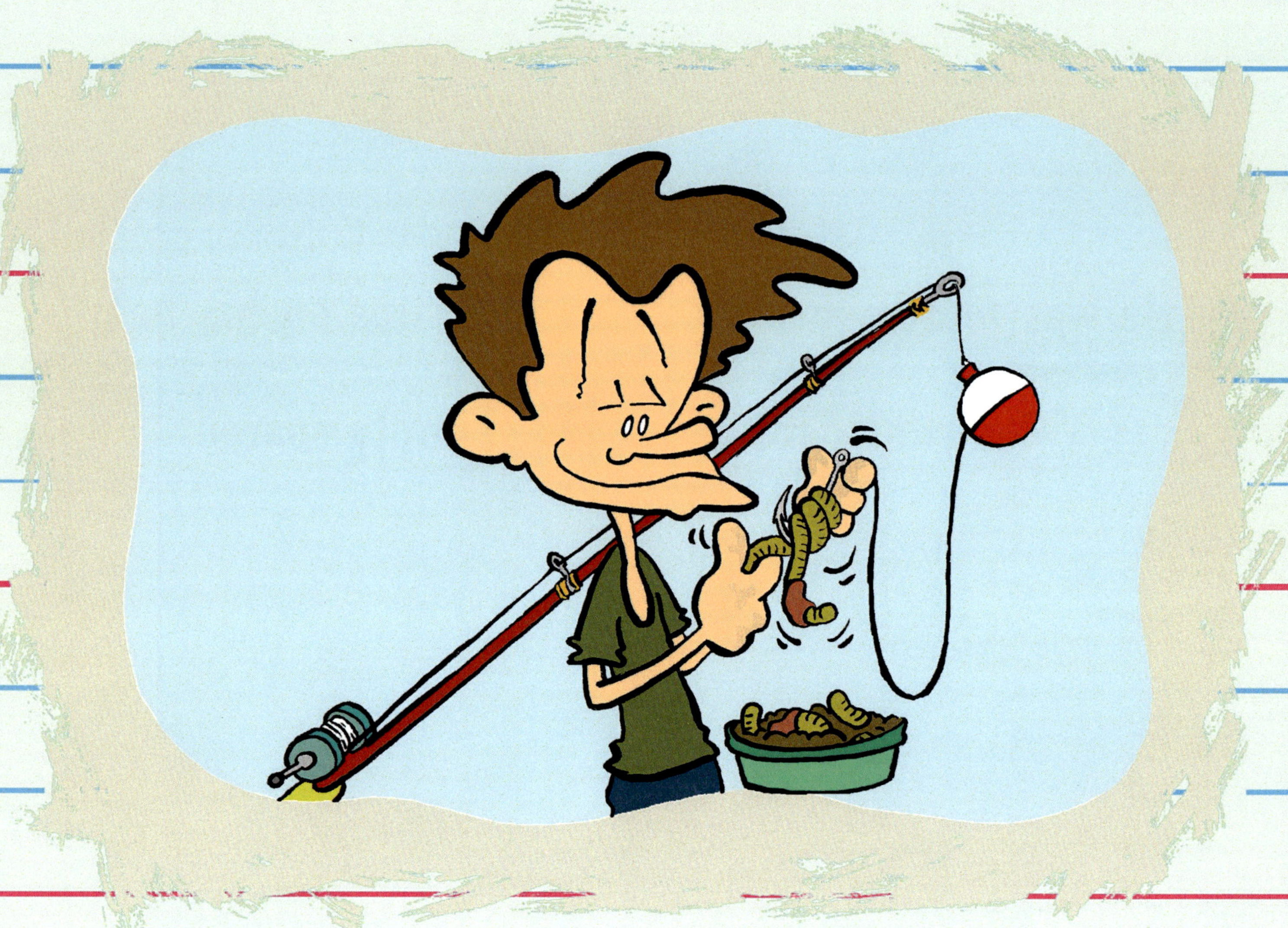

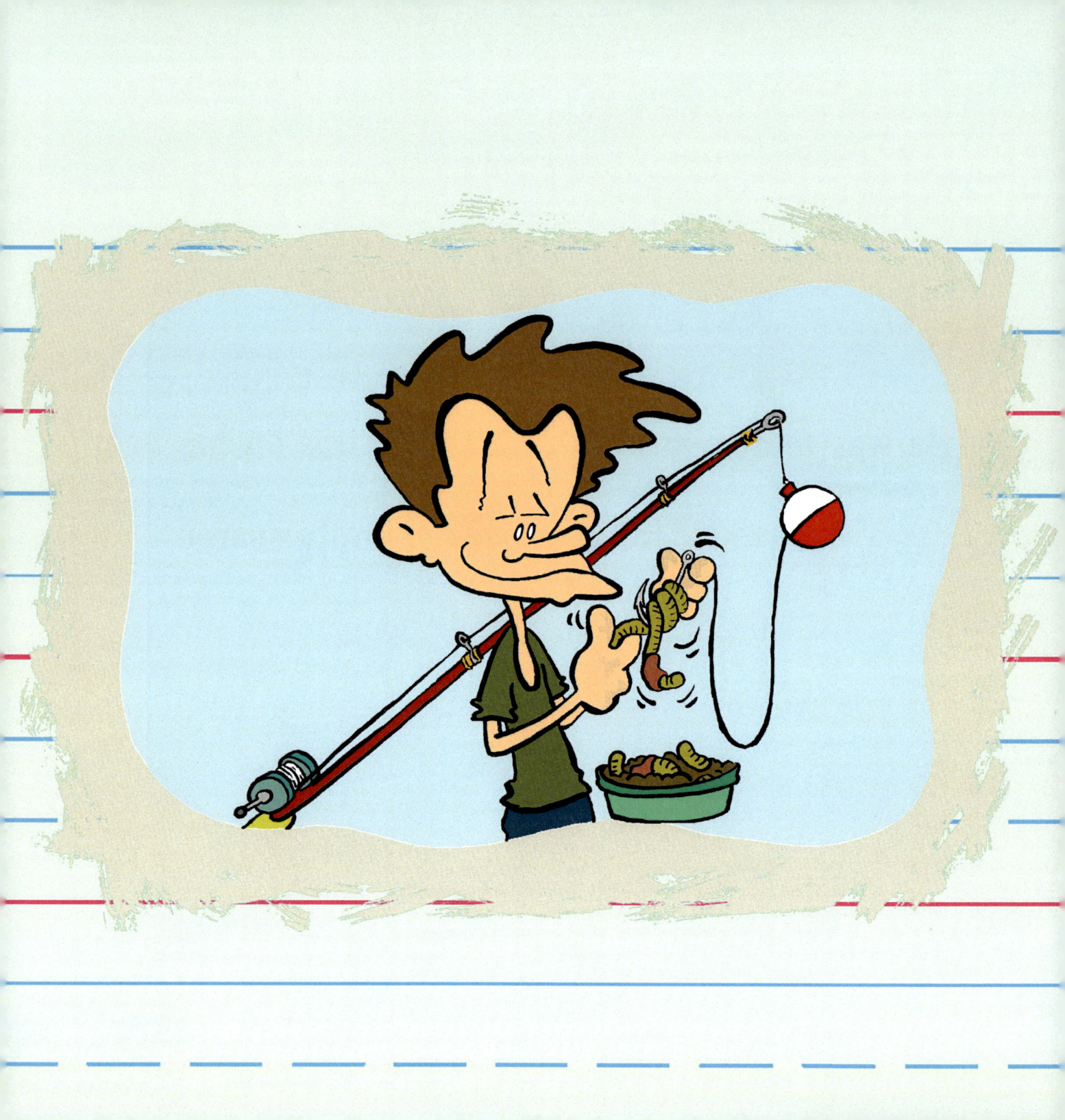

He was the best at putting squirmy worms on hooks.

He was a natural at this! No lessons; no books.

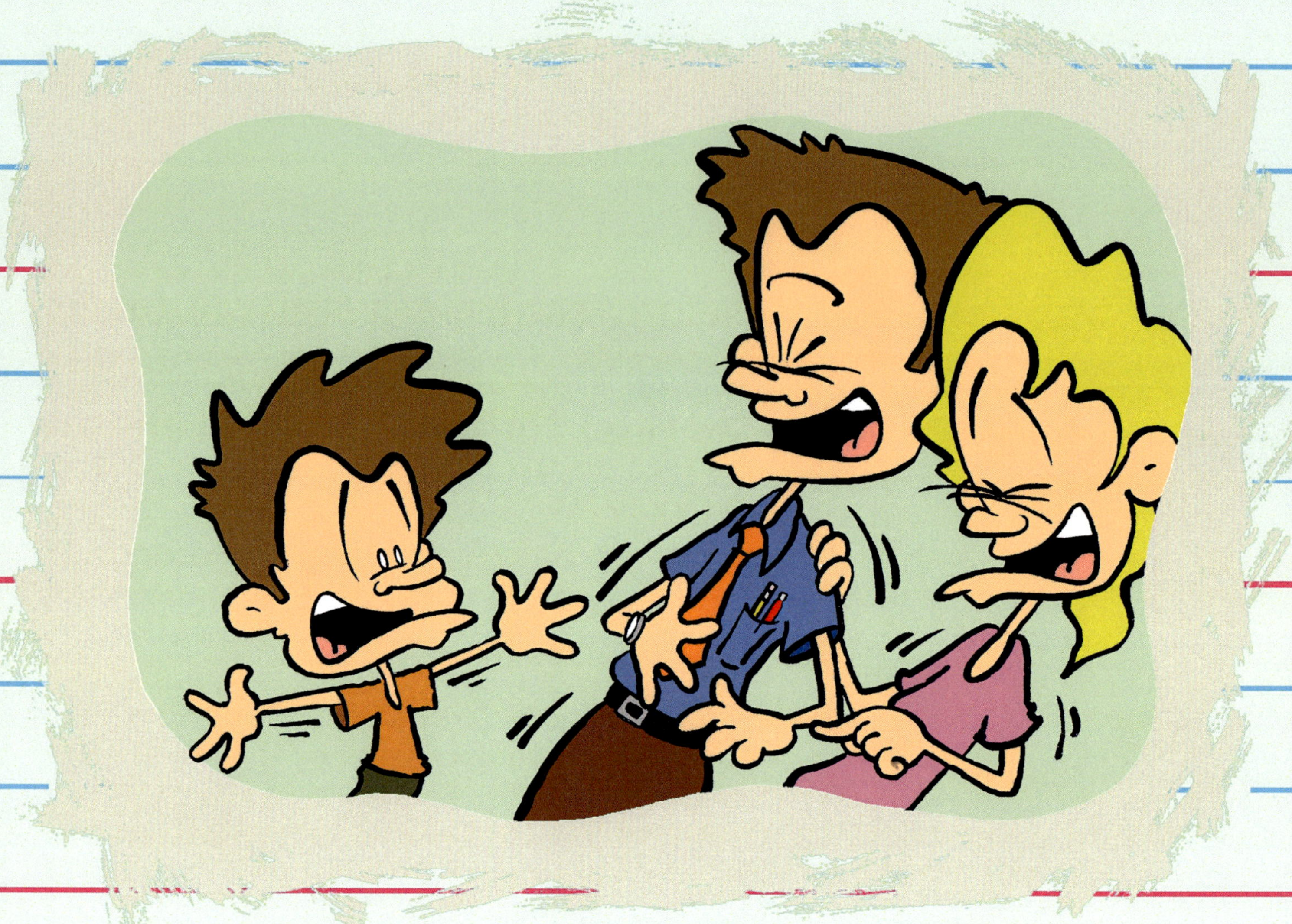

He could even tell funny jokes.

Getting great laughs out of his folks.

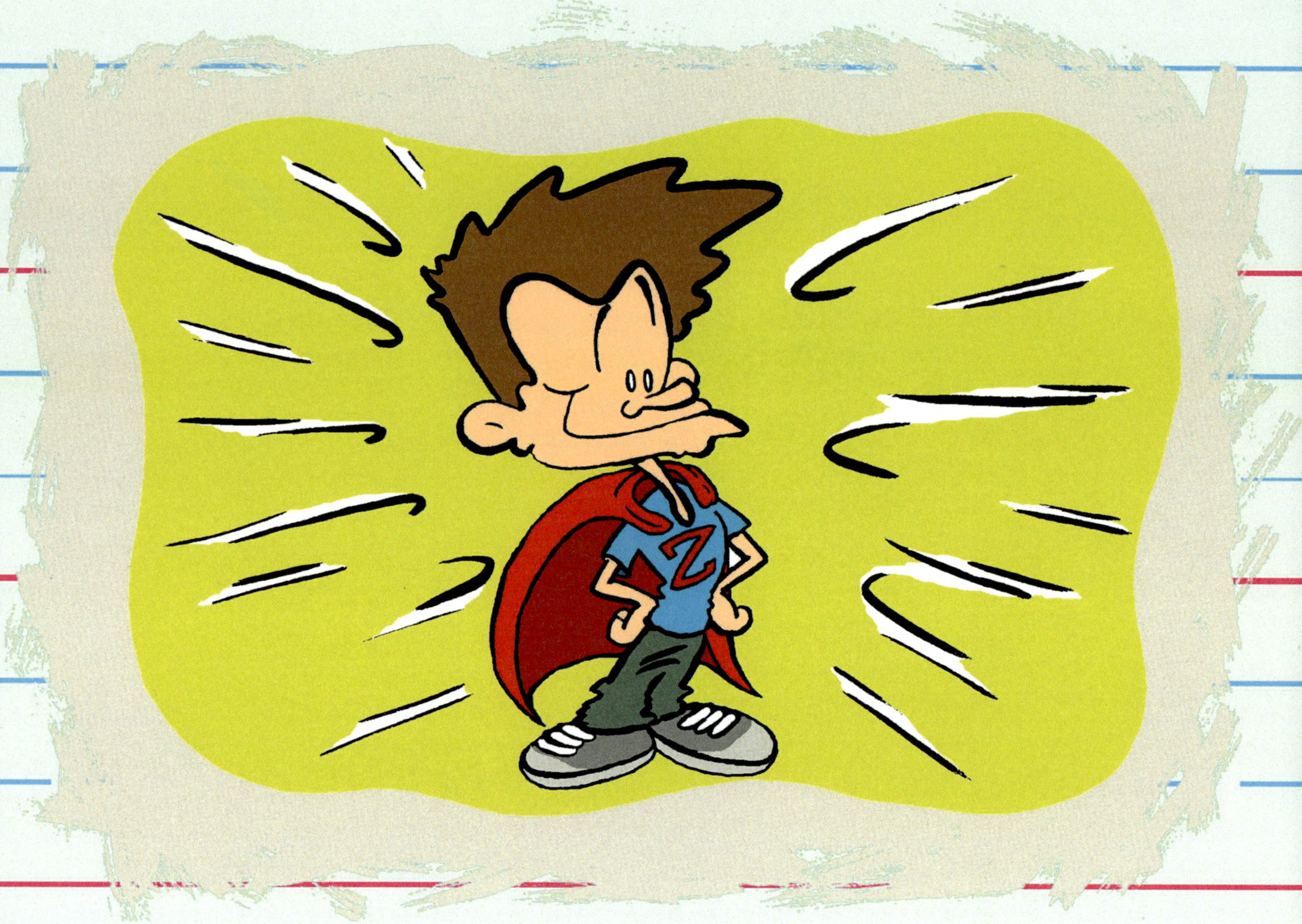

He was so good at everything, he didn't have to try.

He couldn't wait to do these things at school;

Zander wasn't shy.

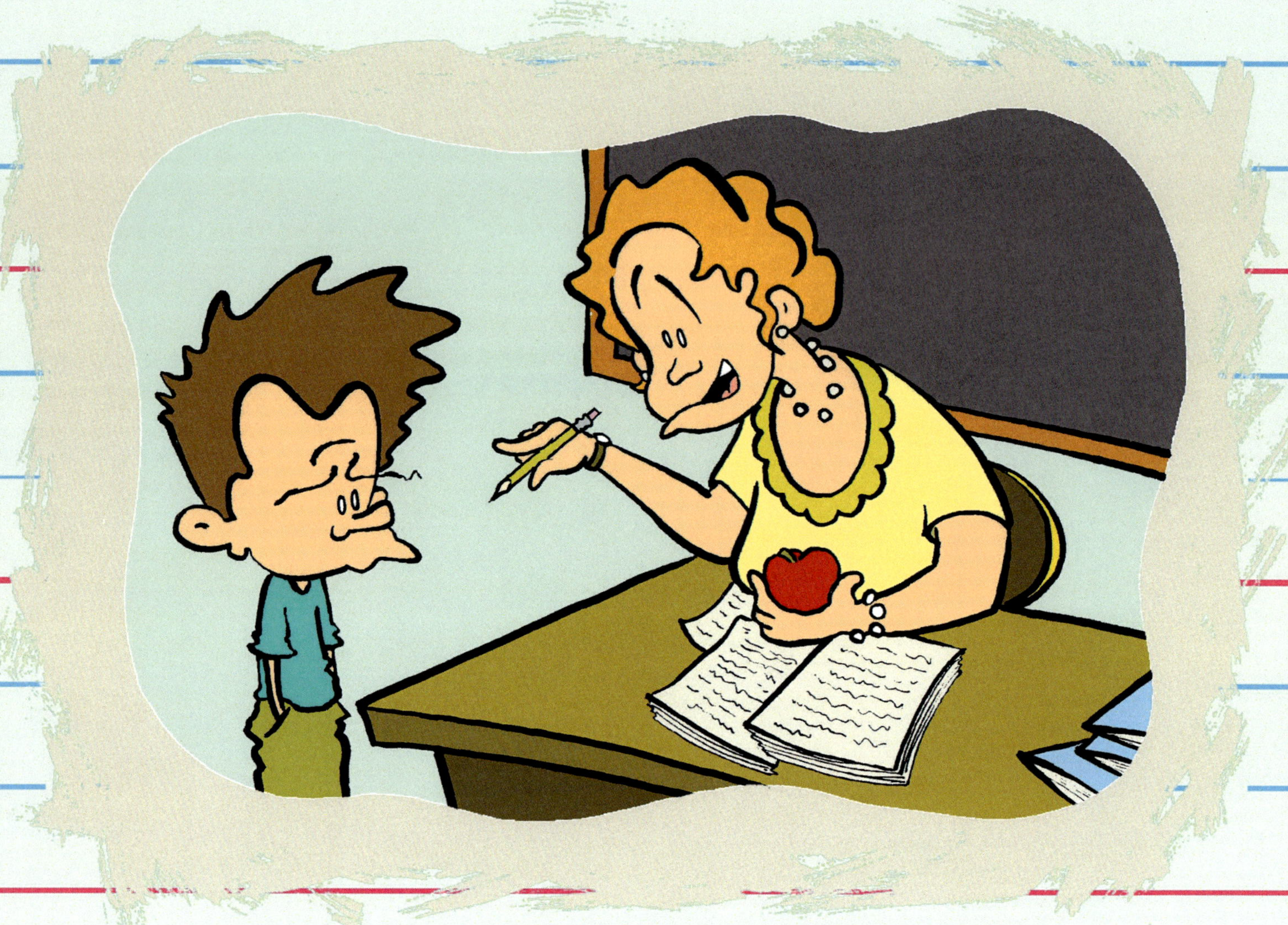

The teacher had some tasks that day
that Zander didn't like.

They weren't as fun as playing catch
or riding his two wheel bike.

"That doesn't matter", Zander thought.
"I can do it all!"

"No matter what the task at hand,
I will have a ball"

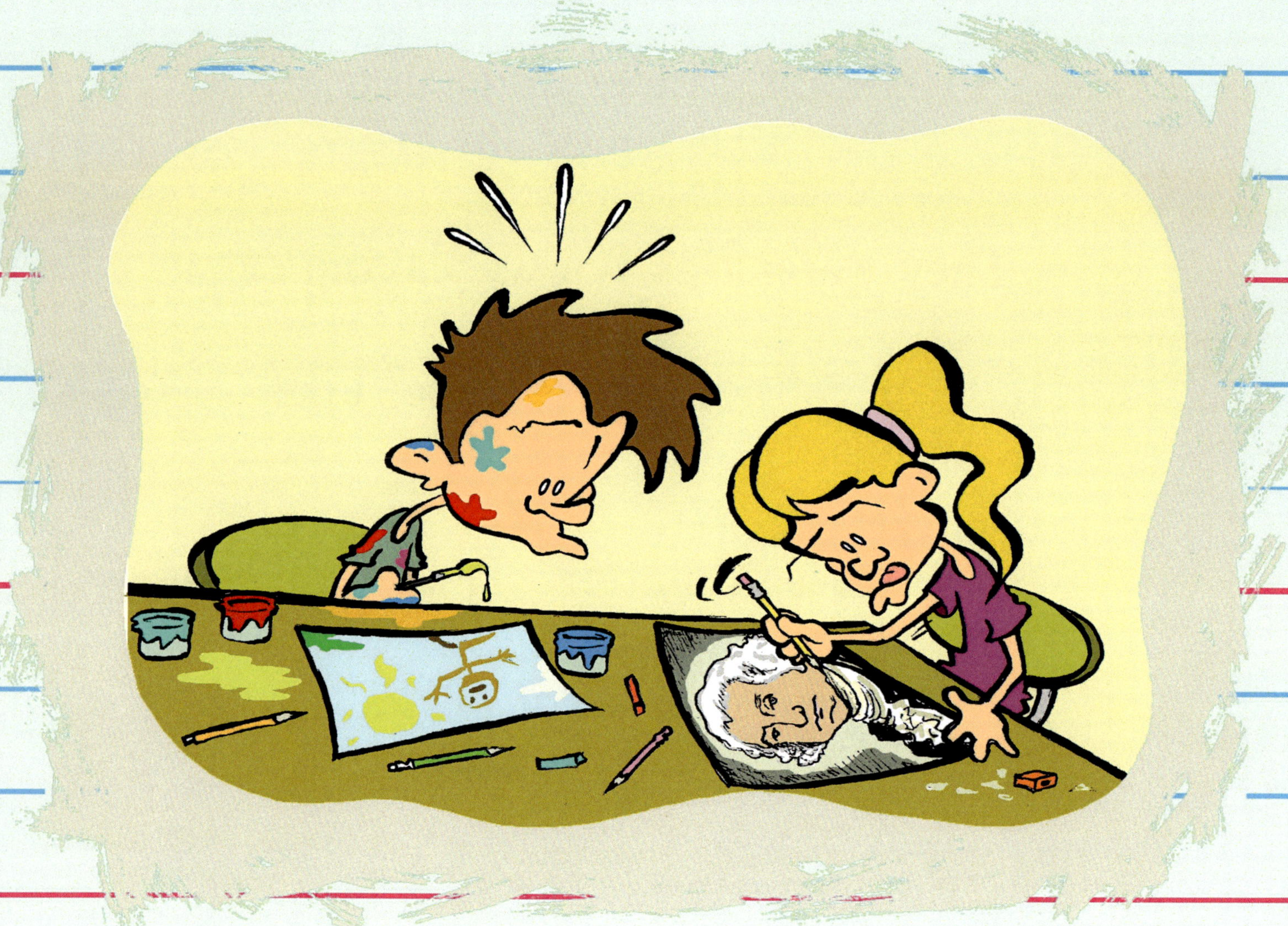

In Art Class, he went to work thinking this was easy to master.

Soon enough his masterpiece showed signs of being a disaster.

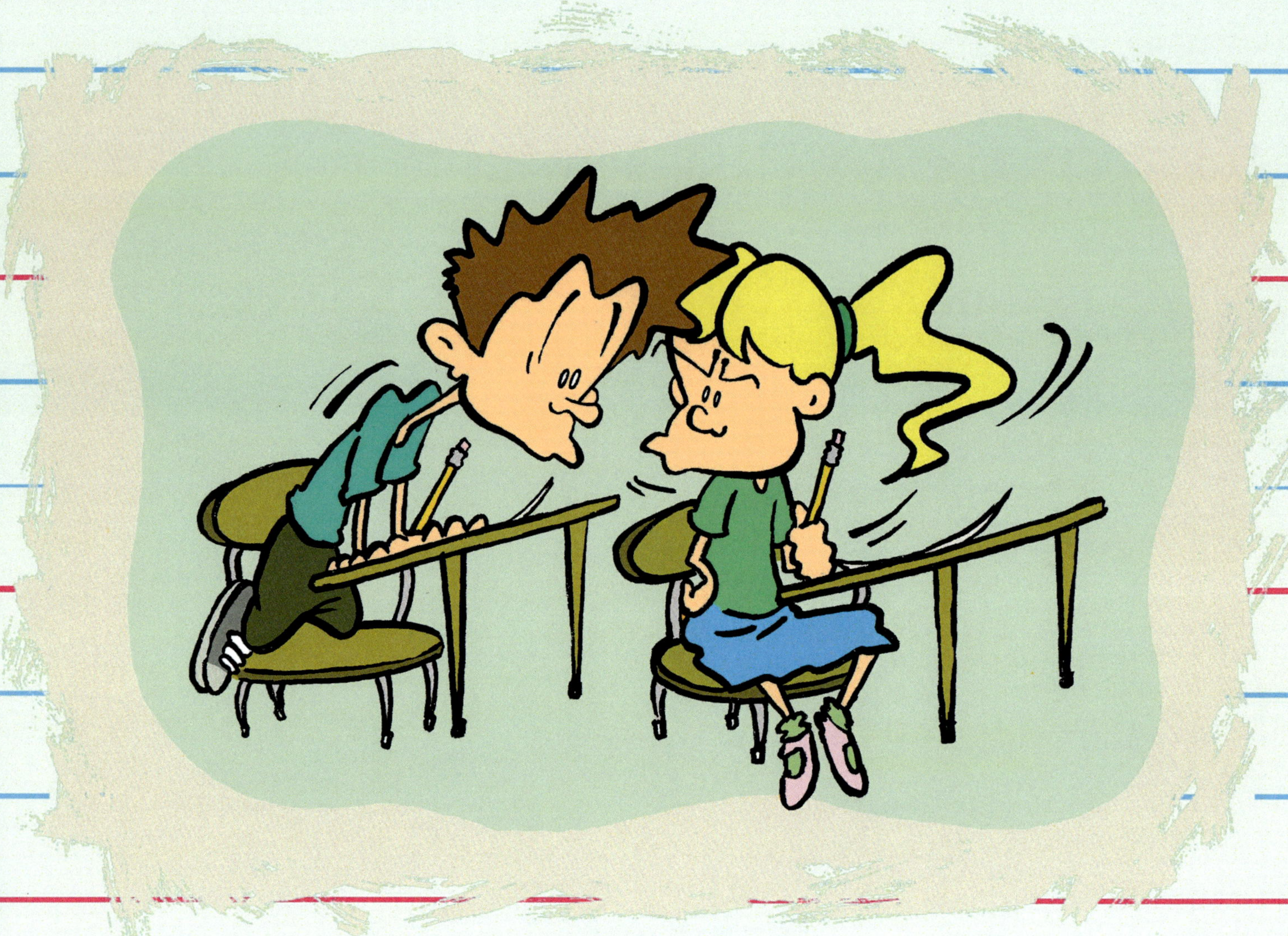

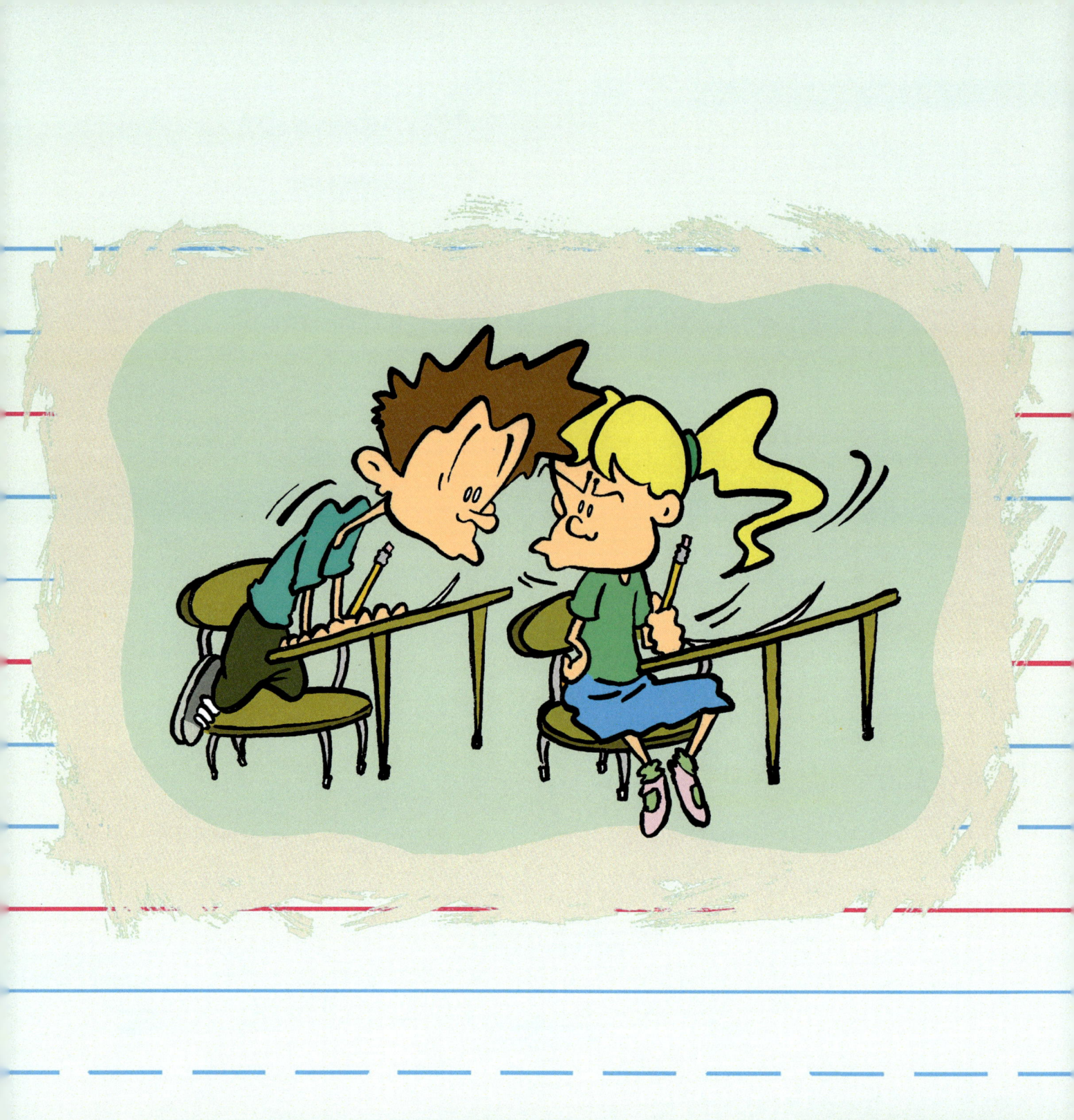

Teacher gave the class a job to do,

Zander started right away.

But something strange happened to him.

His eyes began to stray!

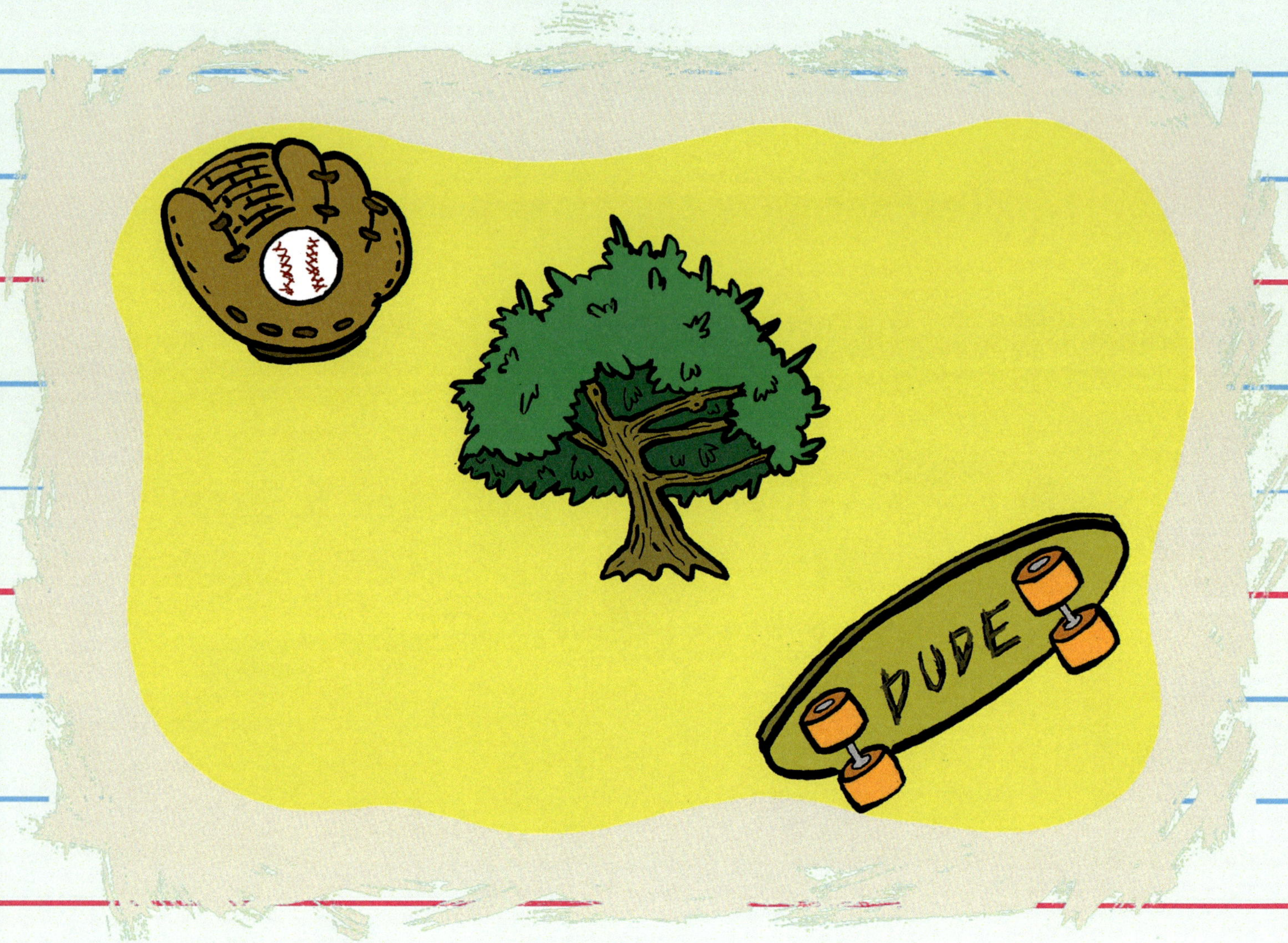
DUDE

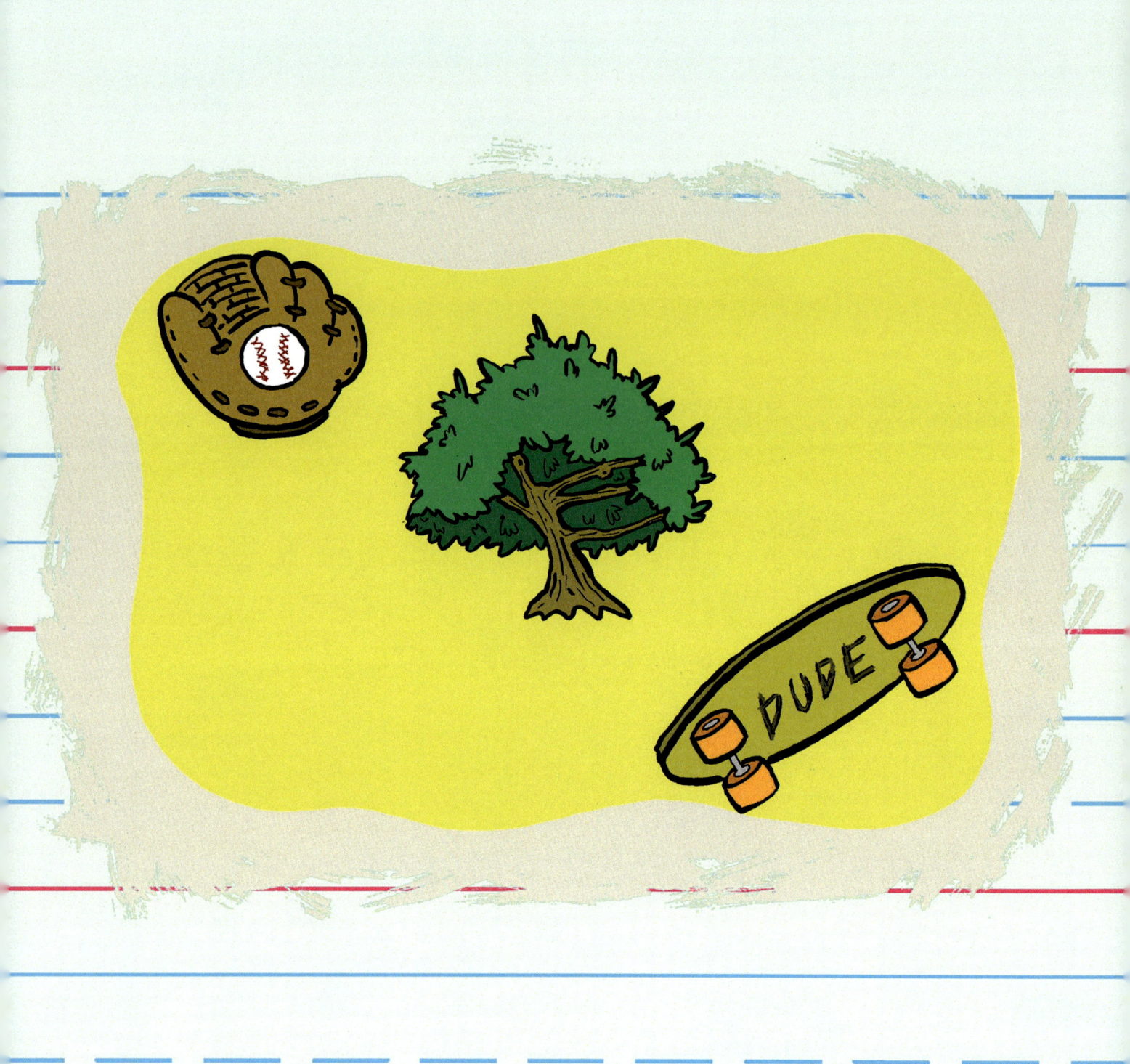

Zander couldn't wait for gym

to demonstrate his skills.

Climb a tree, catch a ball,

or skateboard down some hills.

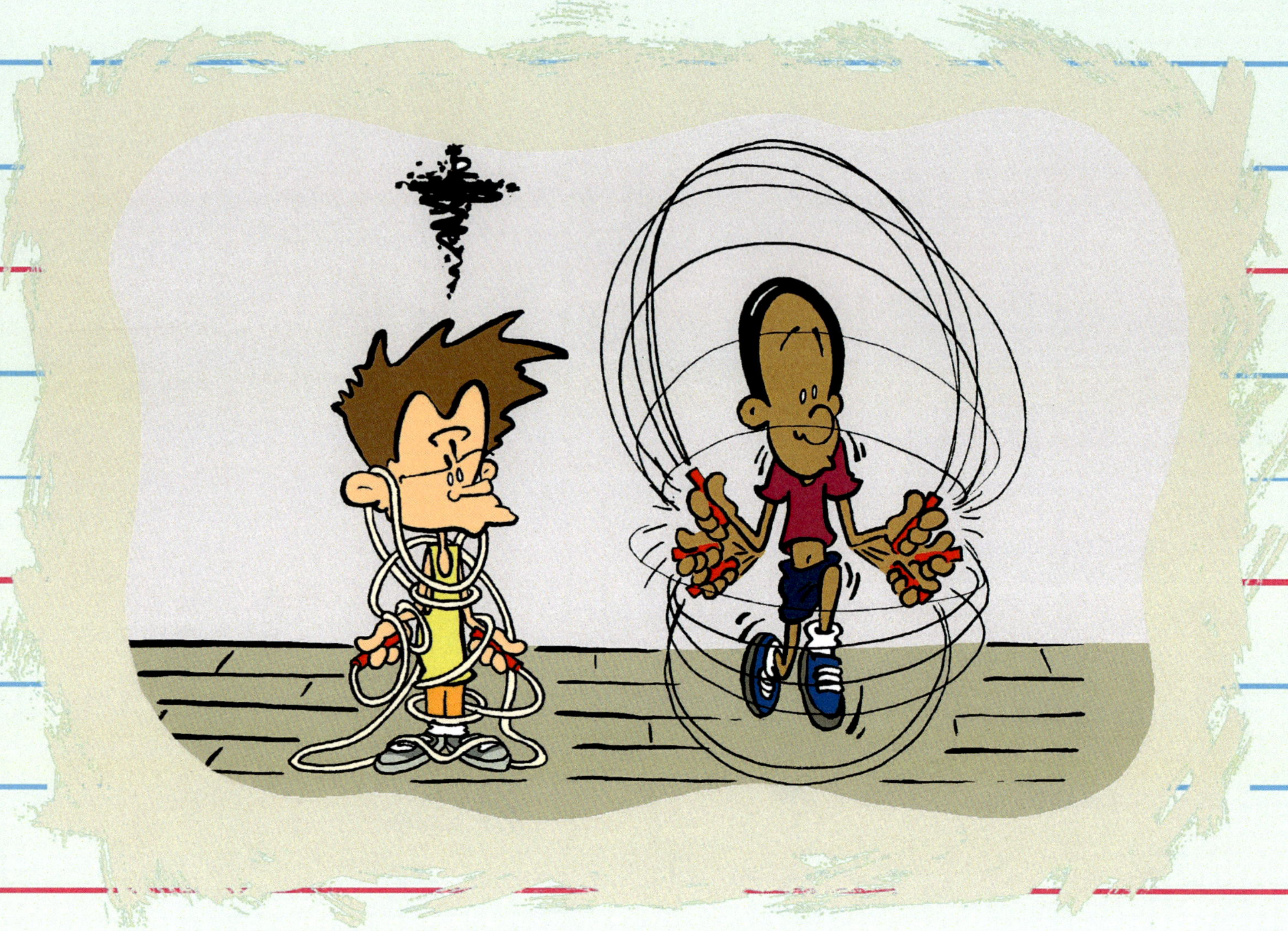

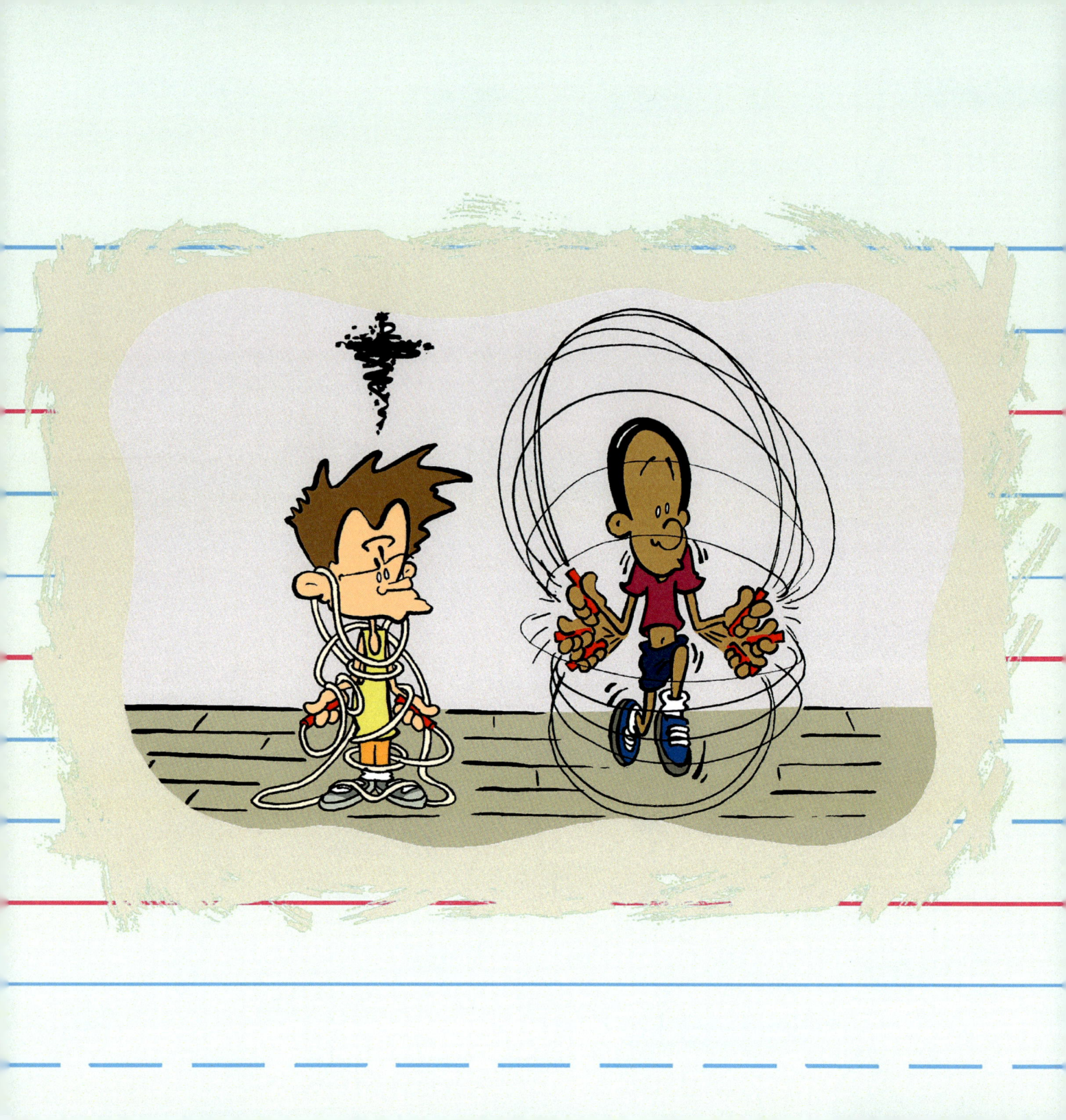

But to his surprise, there was

no board, no tree, no ball.

Just Zander getting all tangled up

-it made him feel so small.

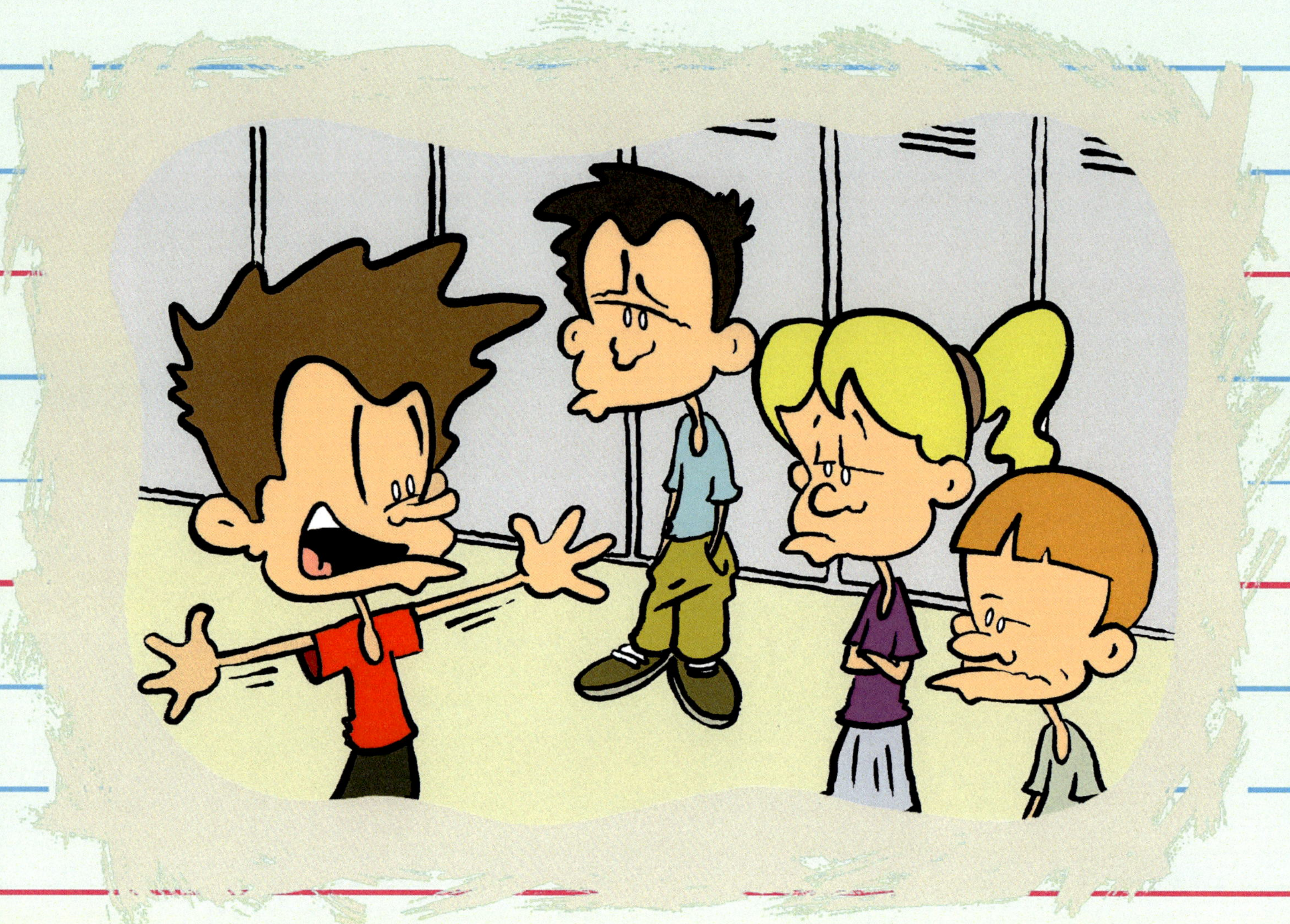

No one laughed at the joke he told
and Zander wondered why.

"When I told that joke at home,
mom laughed until she cried!"

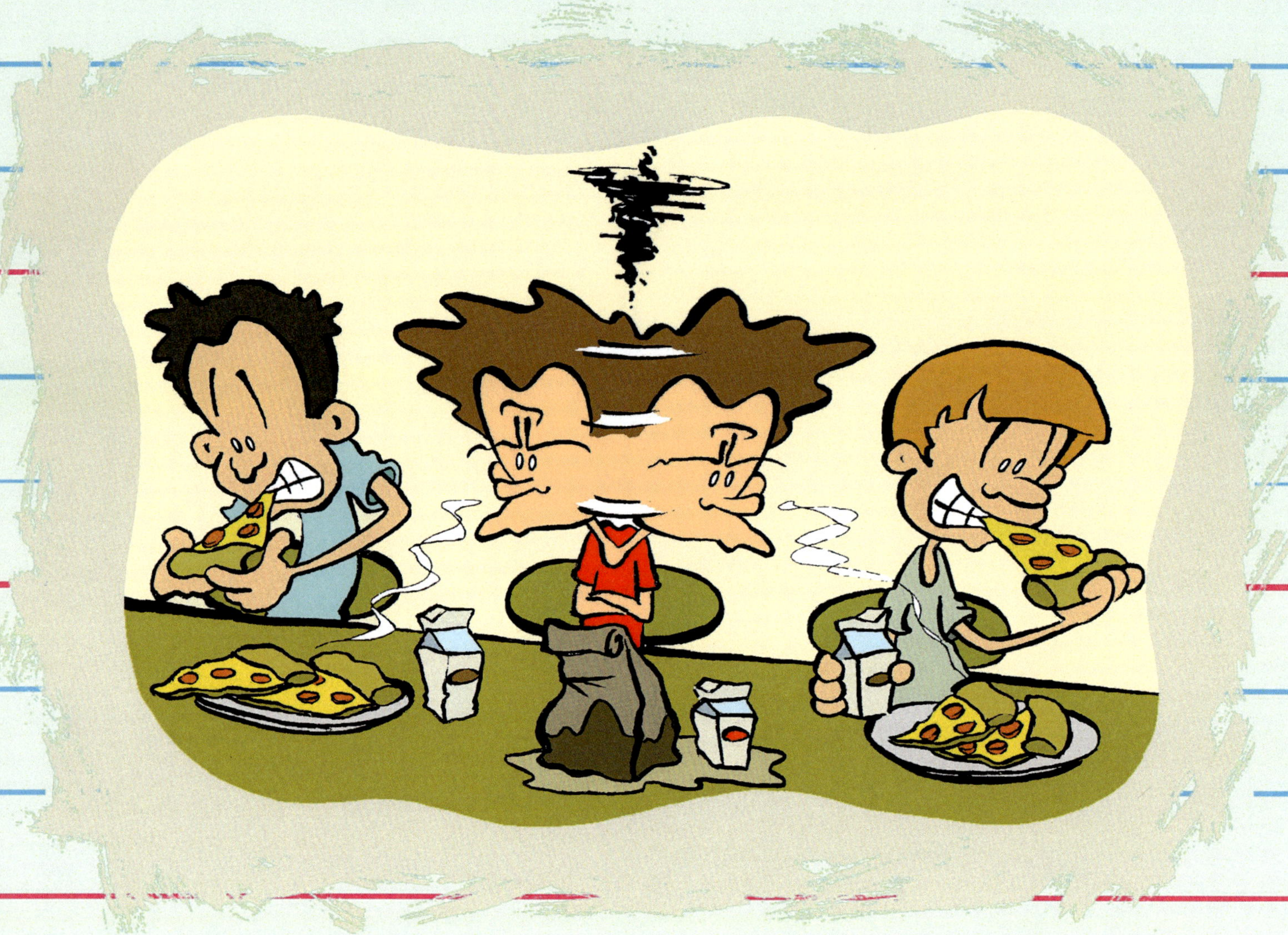

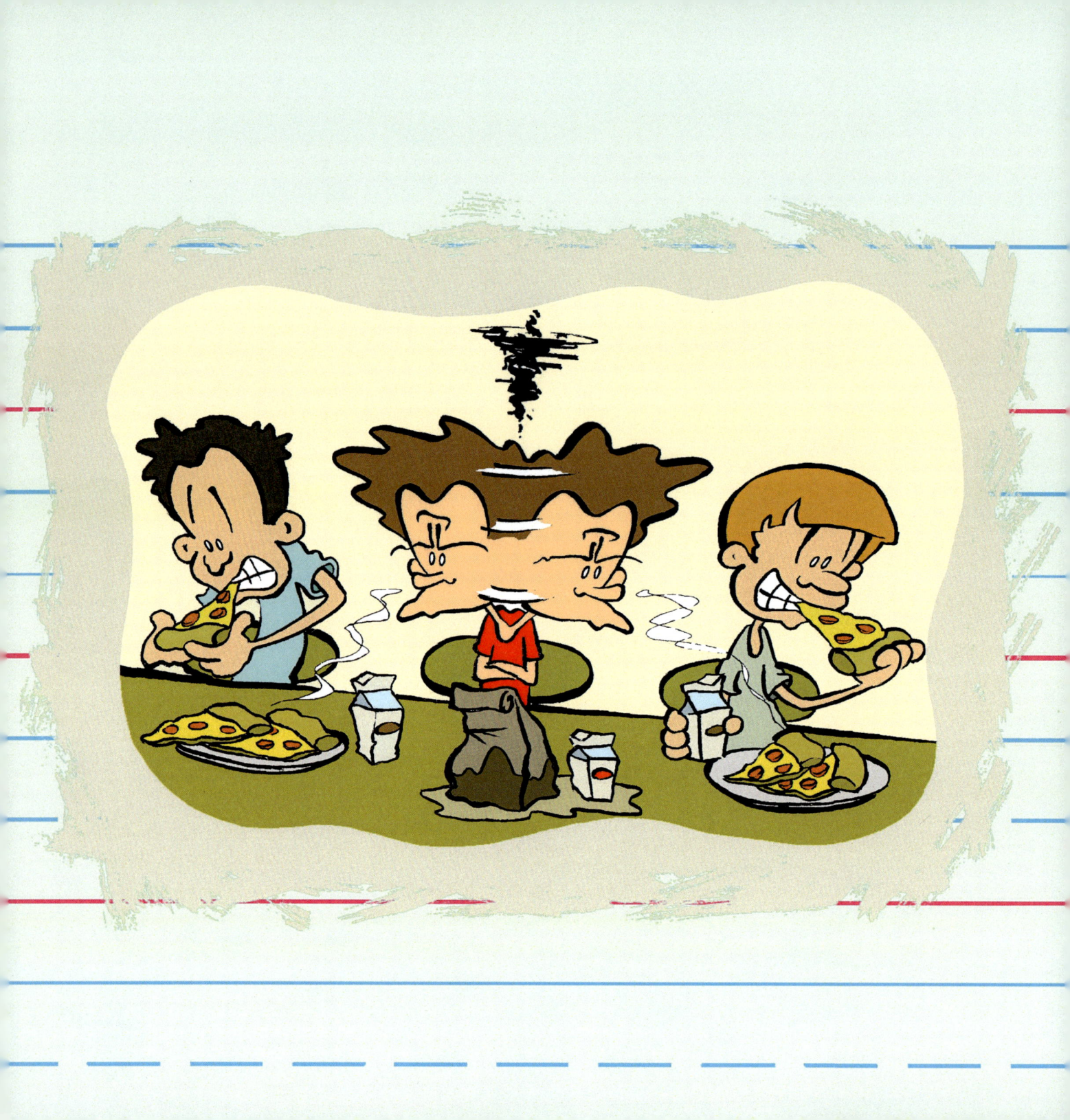

Lunch time had arrived

and his meal was not the same.

"Hey, these guys all have pizza!

My bologna is just plain lame."

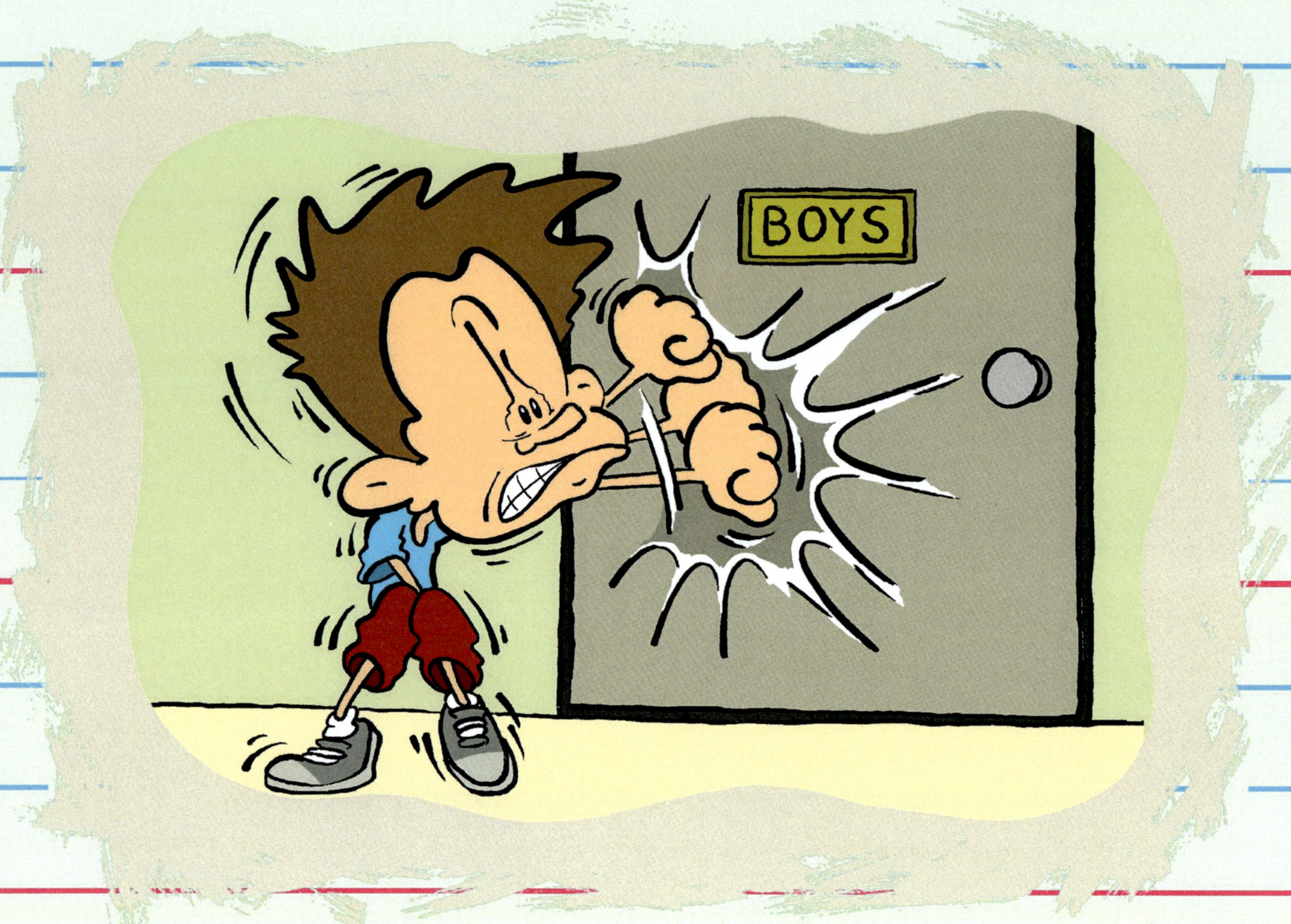
BOYS

Locked doors and taking turns

were not part of Zander's show.

"I have no key,

please hurry up,

I really have to go!"

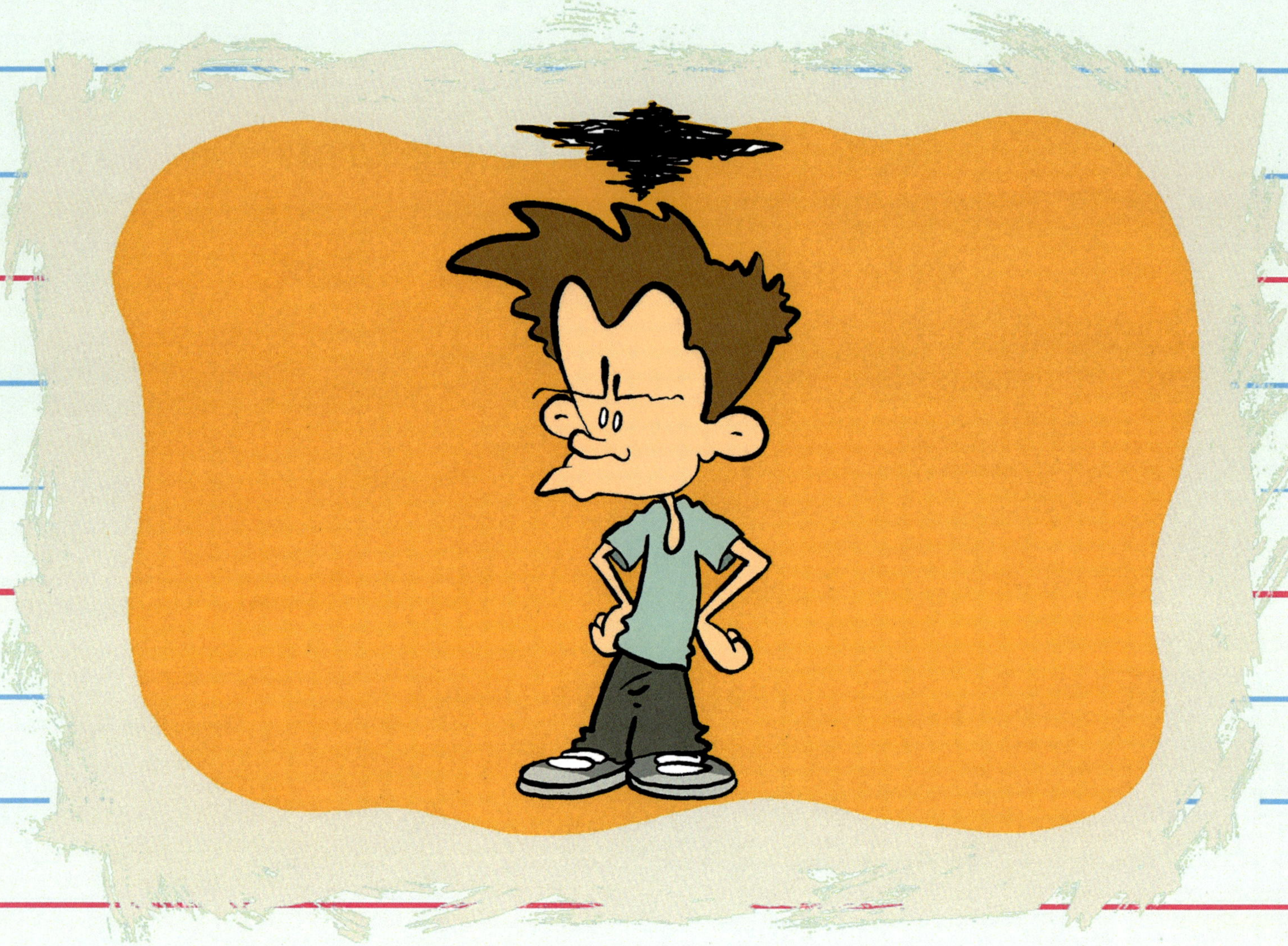

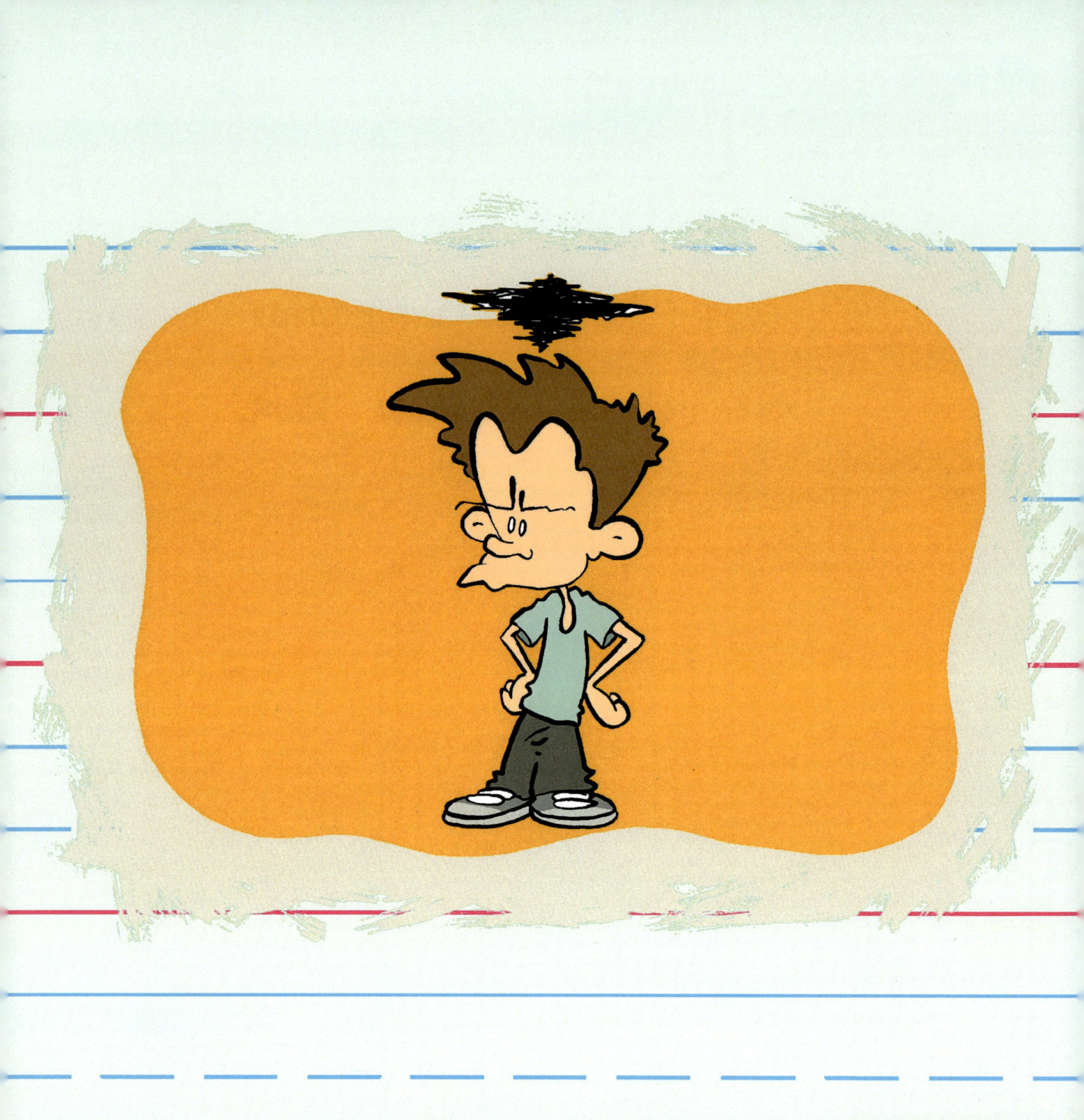

School wasn't what Zander thought it'd be;

where was all the fun?

"Everything I try I fail,

something must done."

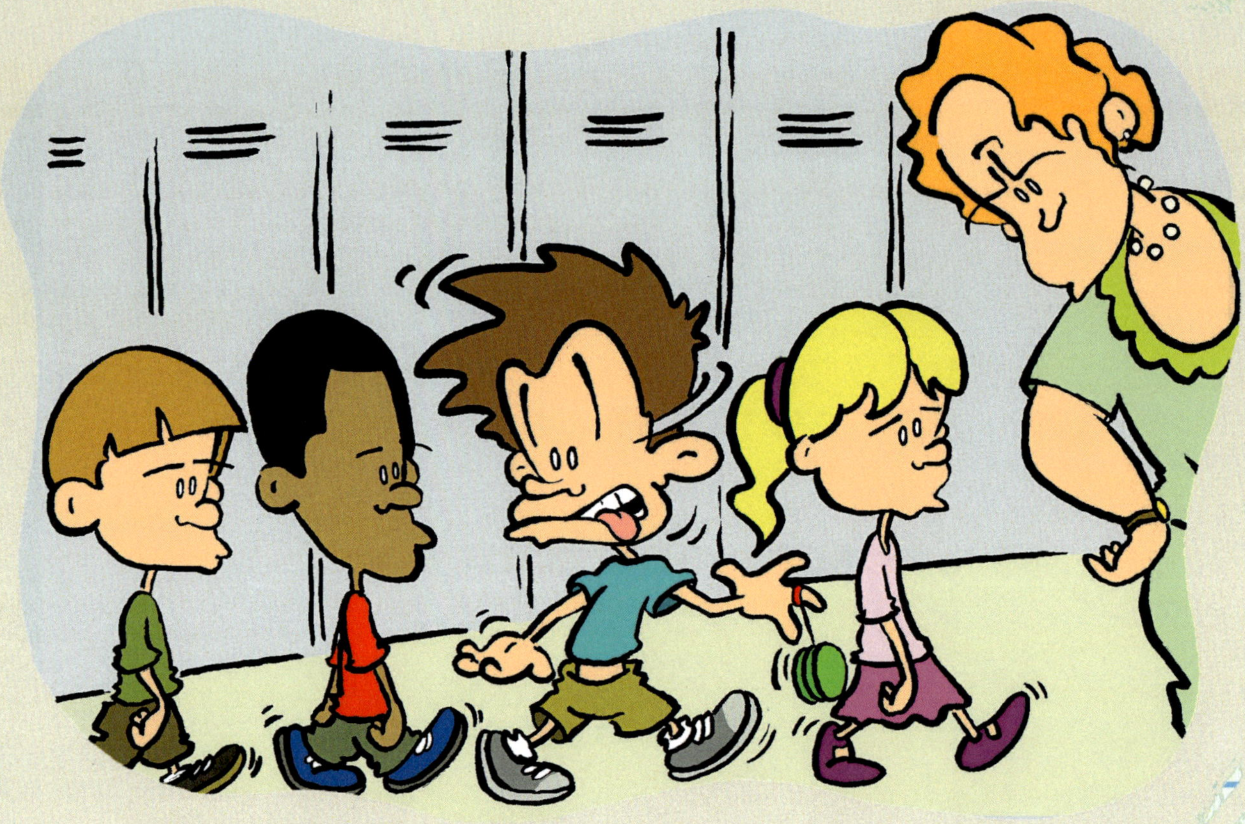

So Zander made a choice

that made the teacher frown.

Instead of listening to directions,

he acted like a clown.

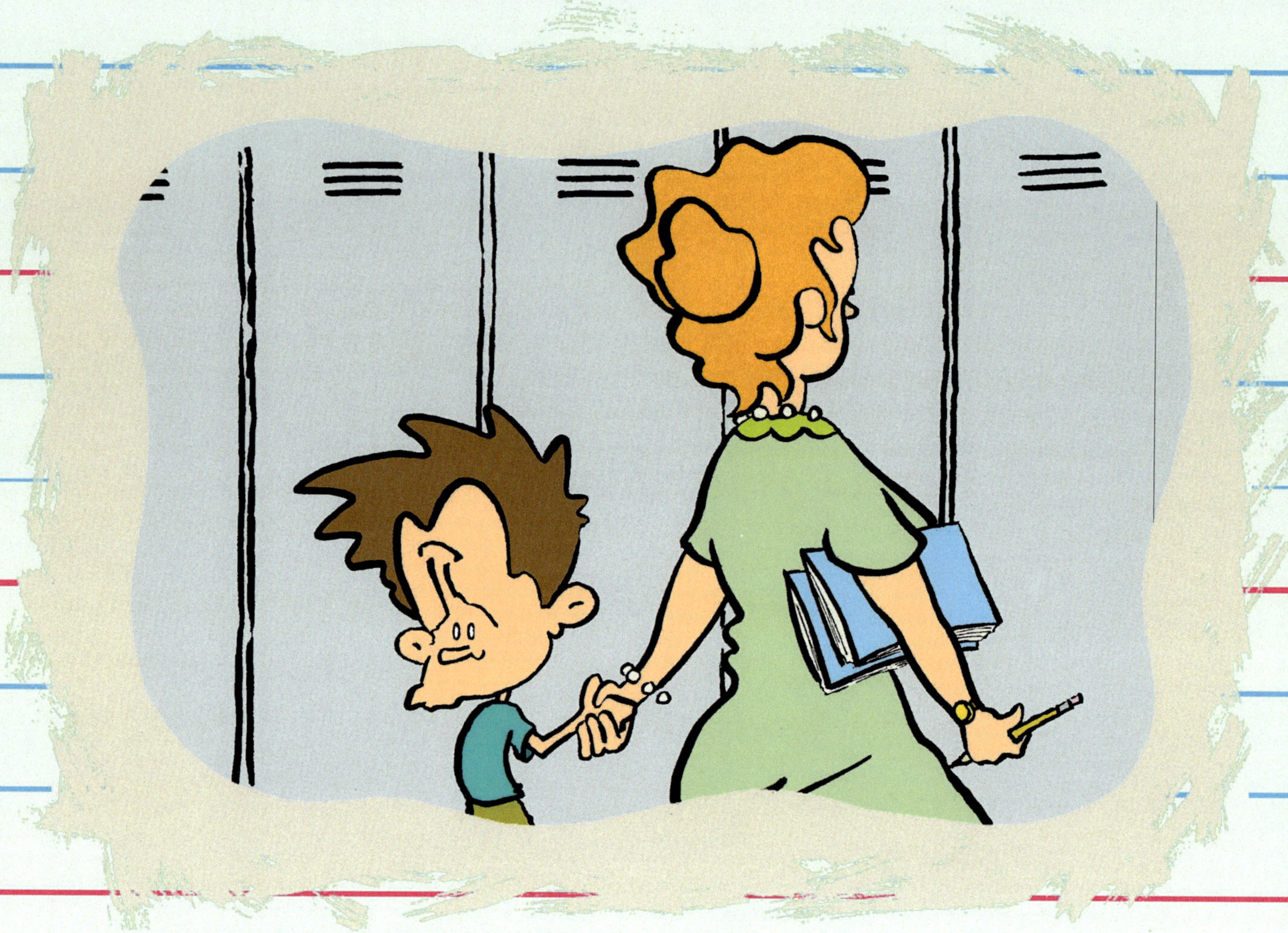

Sadly, down the hallway,

teacher took him by the hand.

He was scared. He was nervous.

He wanted to understand.

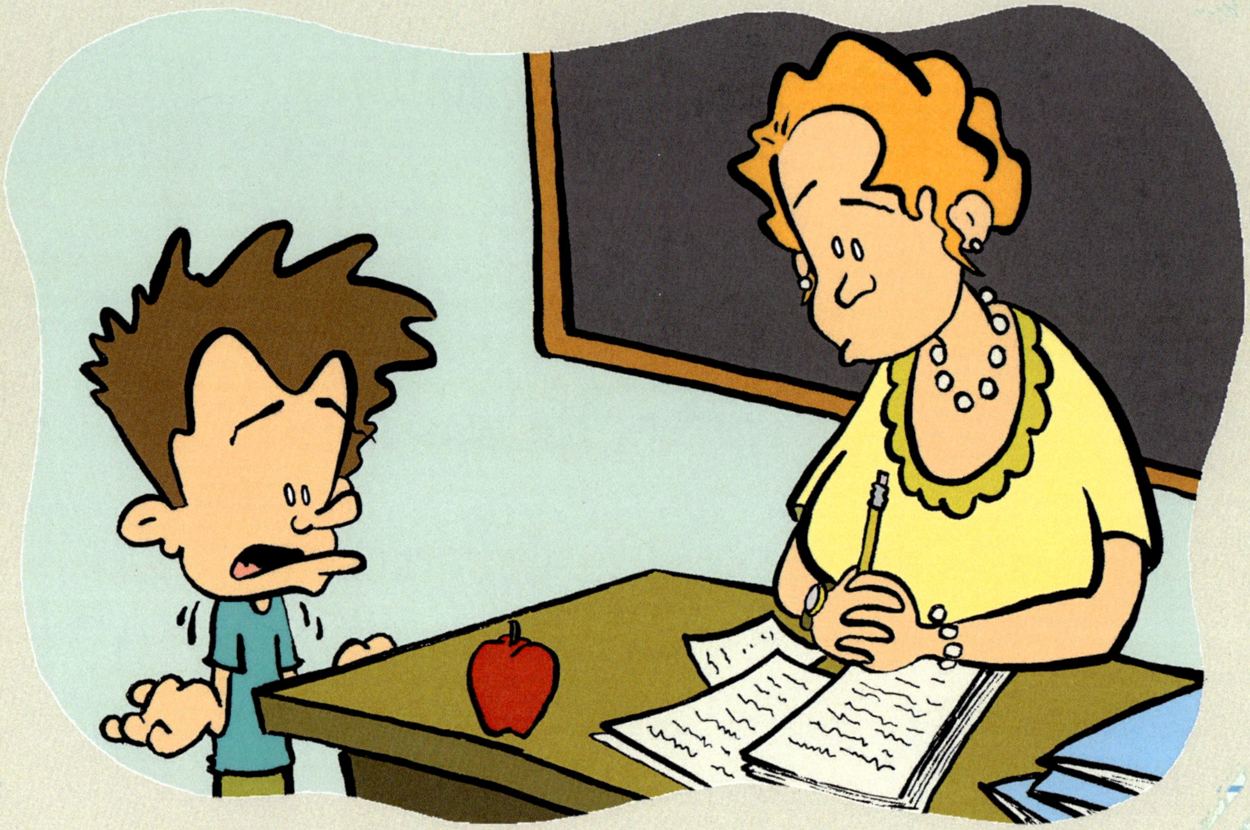

The teacher brought him in the room

and asked him to explain

his feeling of confusion, causing his mental pain.

"Ride my board, catch a ball, nothing's going right.

I can't climb a tree, hook a worm-

- I'm feeling quite uptight!"

"Even going to the bathroom, I'm feeling like a fool.

Level with me teacher - am I even good at school?"

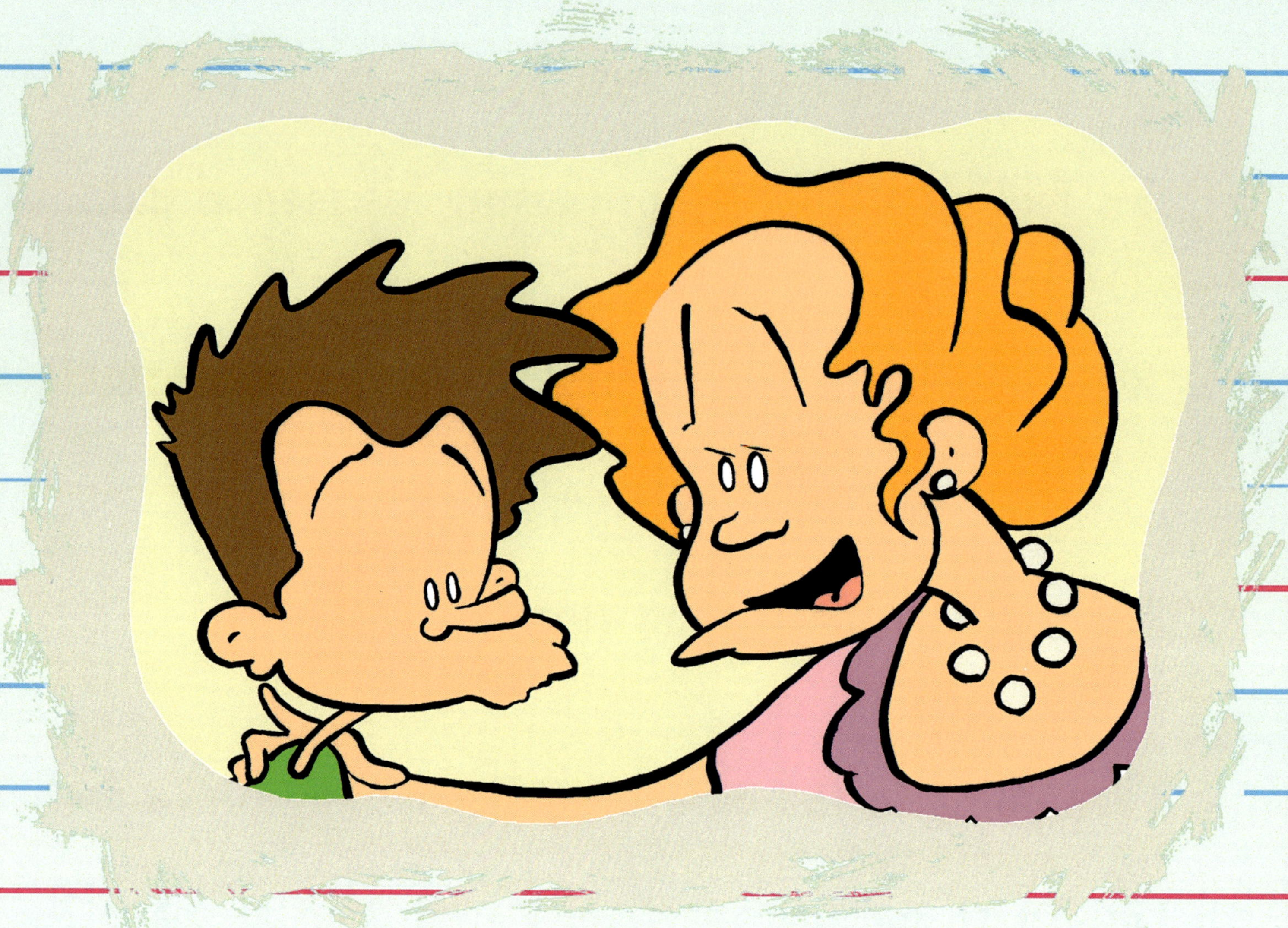

The teacher looked to the sky as if to say "ok".

Guided by her experience, she knew just what to say.

"A baby needs to learn to walk, a pilot how to fly.

All the steps these great skills take,

the first step is to try."

"Don't be mad at yourself if you can't do it right away,

The greatest tasks ever done took longer than a day."

"Any skill takes precious time, regardless, woman or a man

Hear these words NEVER GIVE UP

and I promise Zander can!"

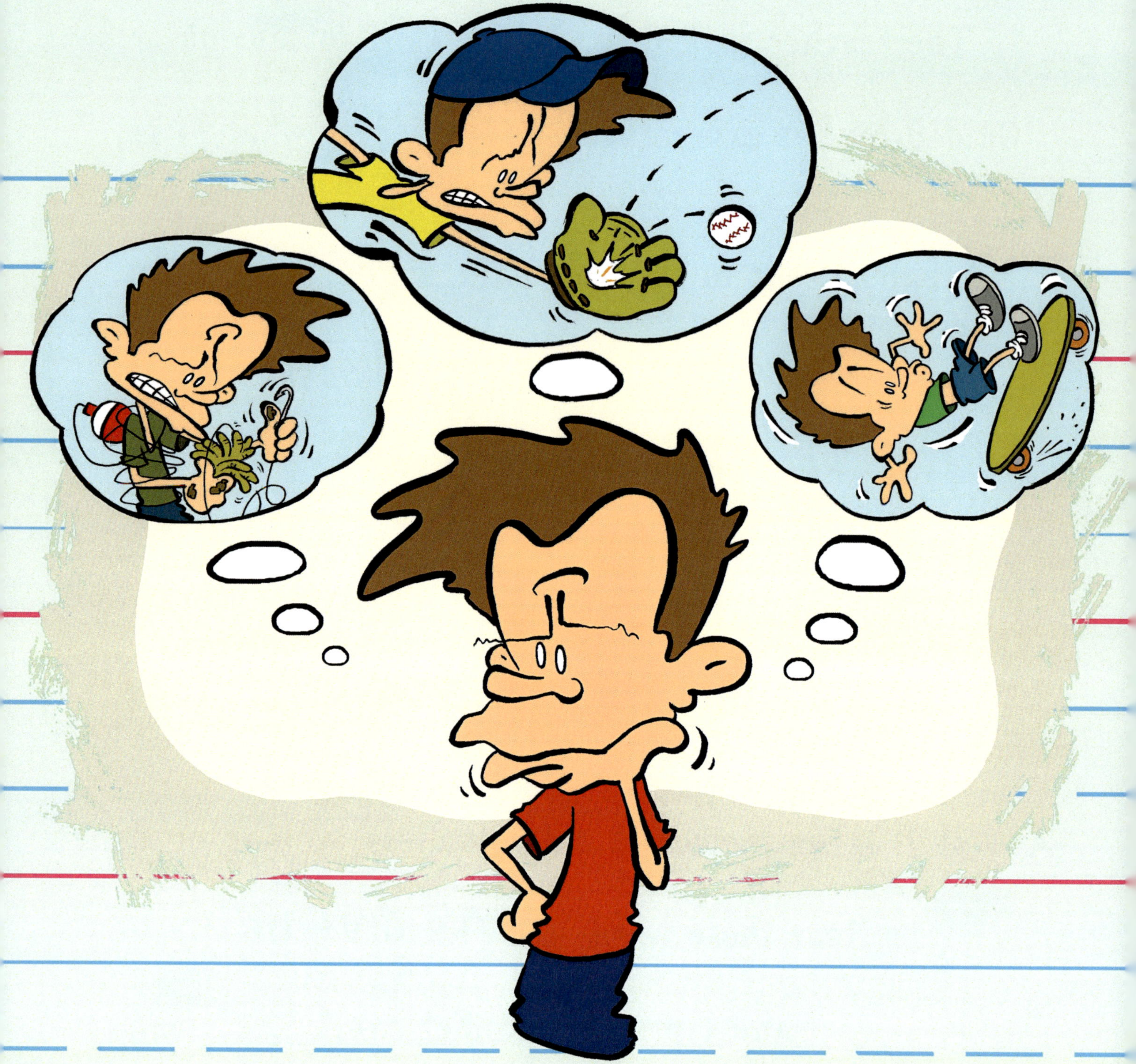

Zander's teacher believed in him,

but he was not so certain.

Every try is like a show

but first you must raise the curtain…

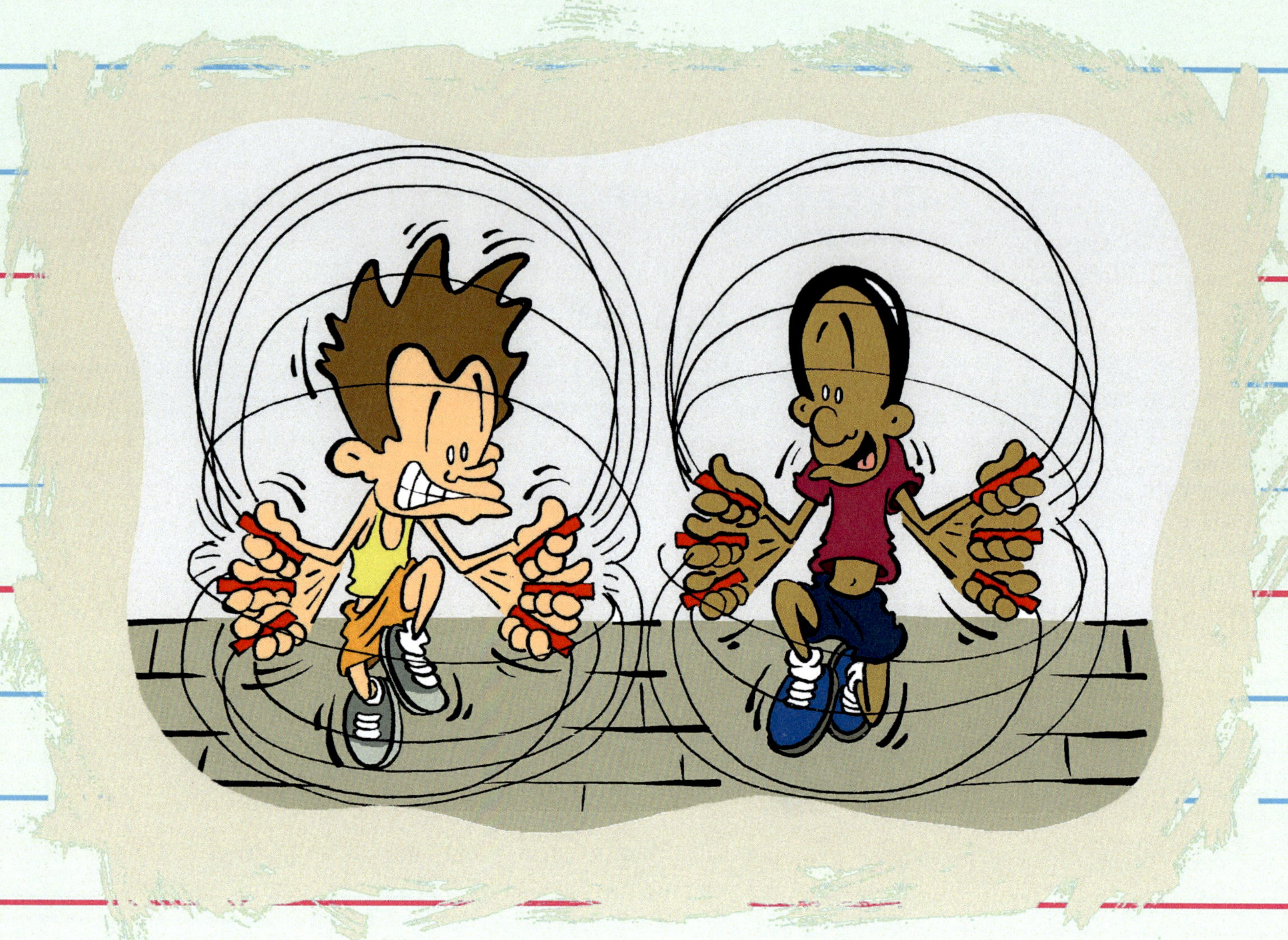

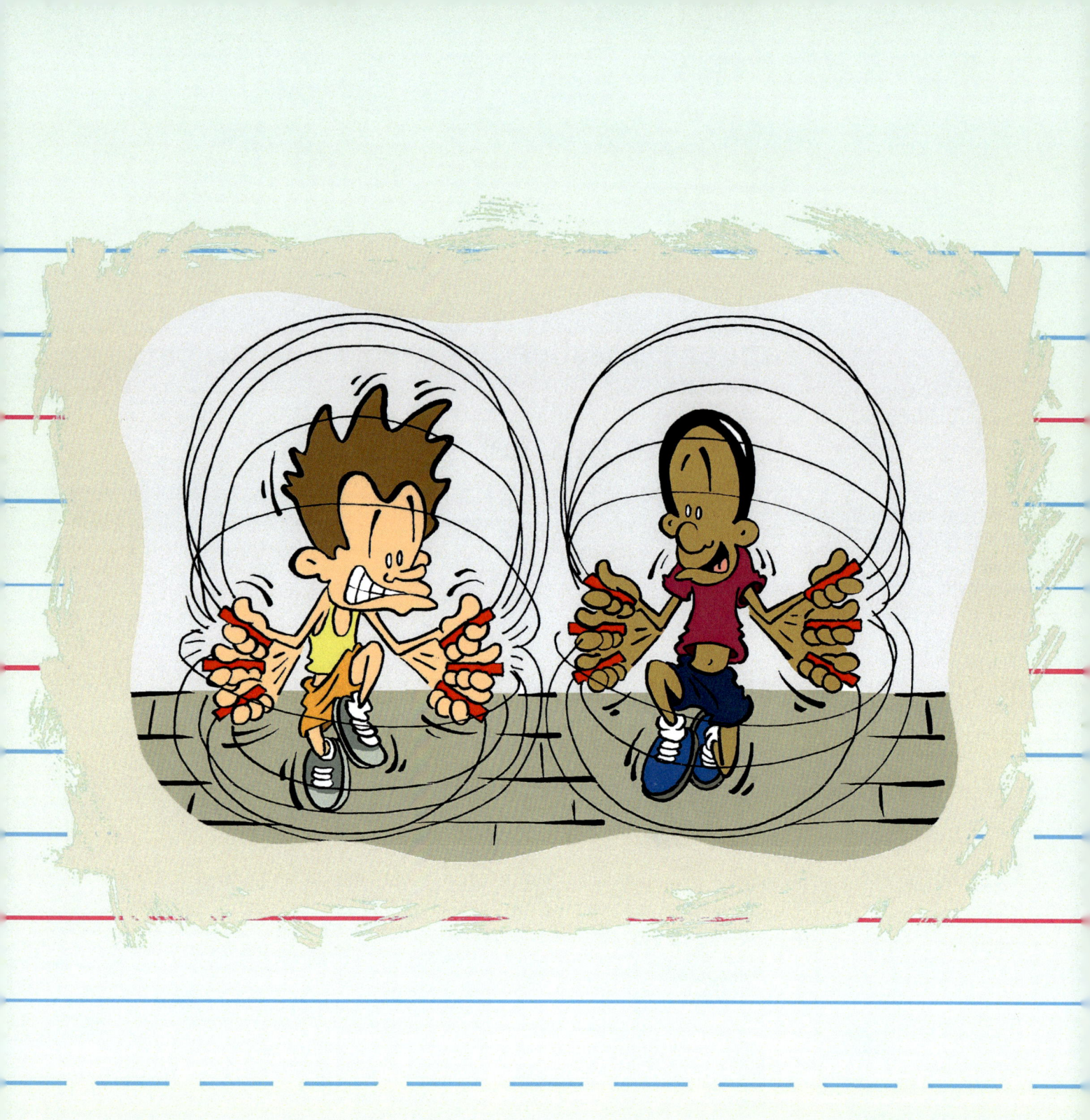

Deciding to start a second act

had really raised his hopes.

He took his time, tried again,

and began to master the ropes.

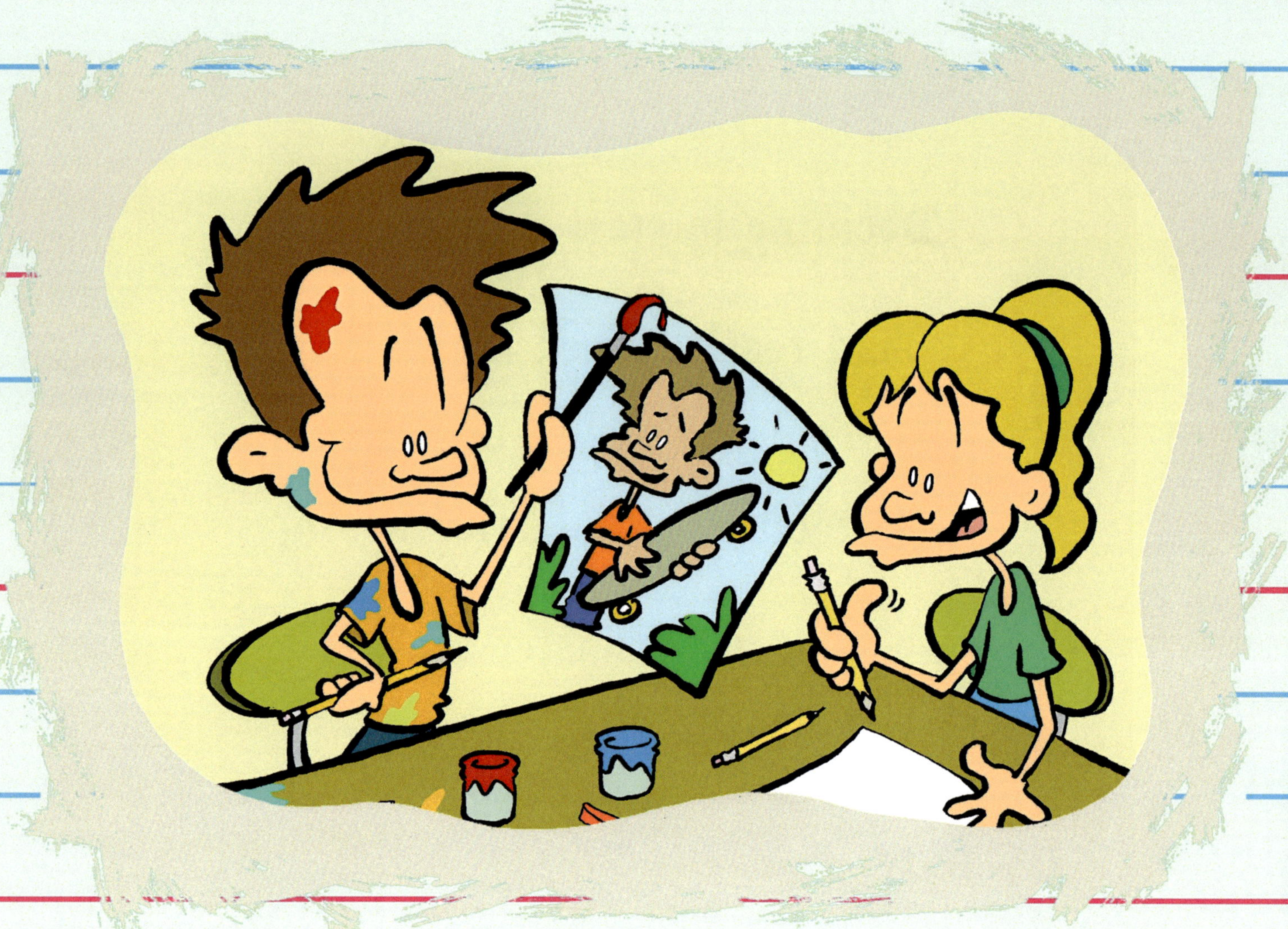

Zander tried to create a piece

that was really an awesome sight.

He took his time and it wasn't bad.

"My teacher must be right!"

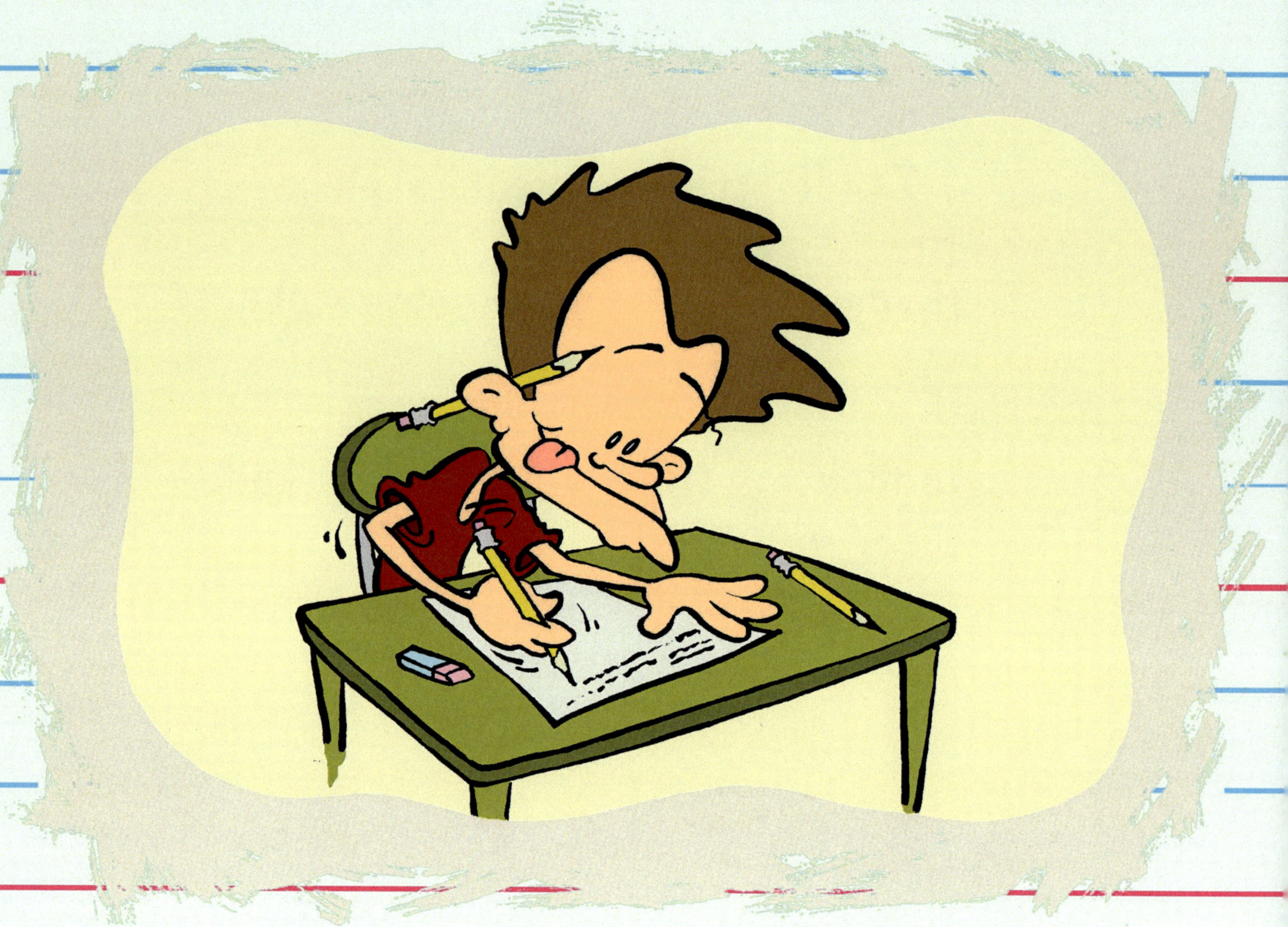

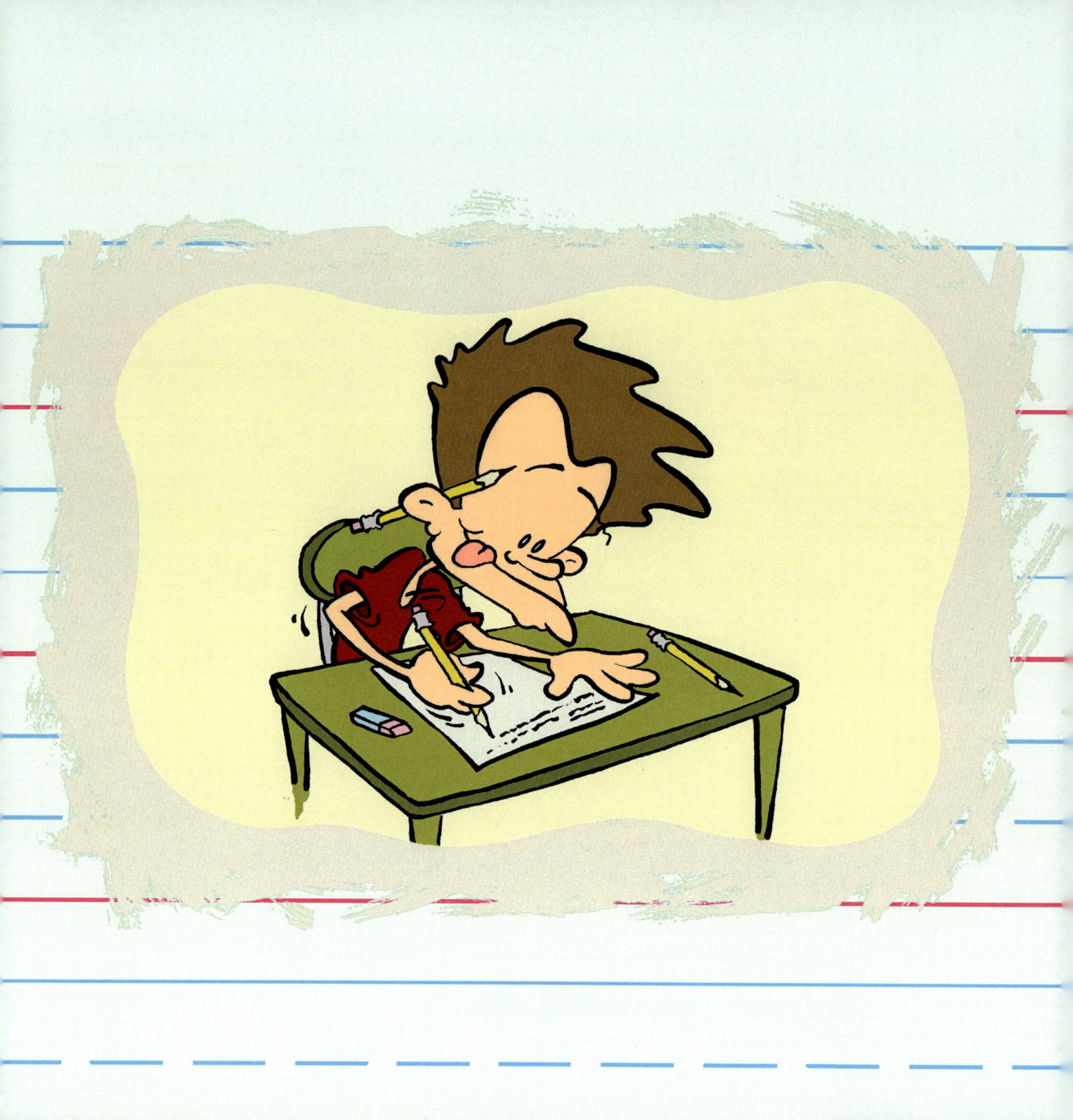

ALWAYS TRY and NEVER GIVE UP

- he began to believe it was true.

This time, when he sat down to work,

he was no longer feeling blue.

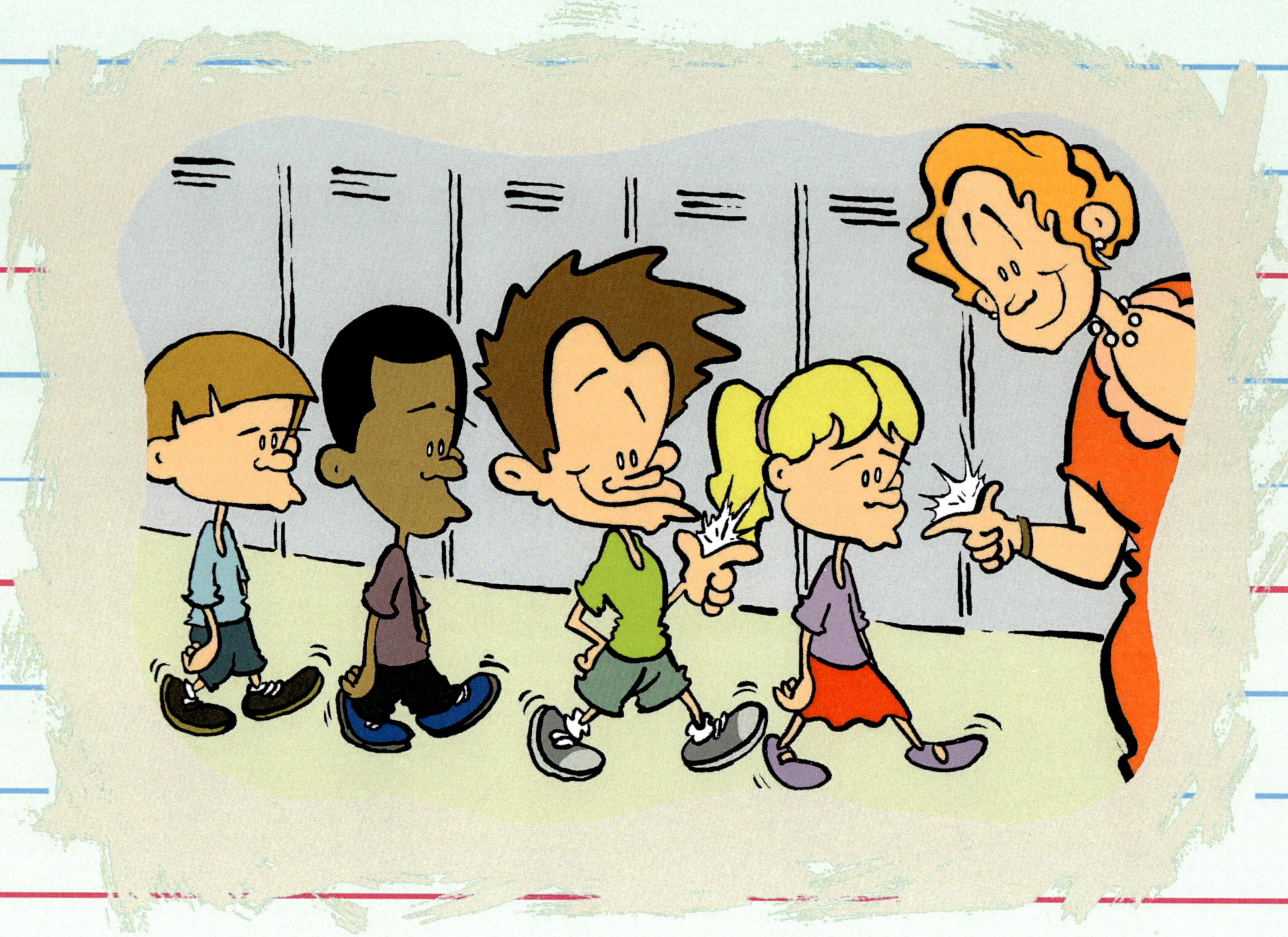

The end of the day was drawing near

as Zander walked down the hall.

With a snap of his hands,

he now understands

when he tries

he can do it all.

ZANDER CAN!

Draw me something new that you can do!

Draw me something new that you can do!

Draw me something new that you can do!

Draw me something new that you can do!

Draw me something new that you can do!

Draw me something new that you can do!

Made in the USA
Lexington, KY
28 December 2017